2nd card

SMI   Smiley, Jane

         Barn blind

BARN
BLIND

HARPER & ROW, PUBLISHERS

NEW YORK

Cambridge
Hagerstown
Philadelphia
San Francisco

London
Mexico City
São Paulo
Sydney

BARN BLIND

A Novel by

JANE SMILEY

40,468

FIRST EDITION

Library of Congress Cataloging in Publication Data

Smiley, Jane.
  Barn blind.
  I. Title.
PZ4.S6387Bar [PS3569.M39]   813'.54   79-3417
ISBN 0-06-014016-X

80 81 82 83 84 10 9 8 7 6 5 4 3 2 1

To my mother
Frances Graves Nuelle

EVERYTHING was a mess, especially in the dark. By the time he'd negotiated the boot-, book-, whip-, and curry-comb-strewn hallway to the bathroom, and groped gingerly around all kinds of bottles for the light, twelve-year-old Henry Karlson was wide awake. It was then he heard the gentle slap of the back screen door being closed by a human hand, and so, instead of flipping the switch, he went to the window and peered out. His brother John, fifteen, was standing in the moonlit driveway, where he had no business. Henry glanced quickly over his shoulder, toward the dark doorway and the other rooms, but his mother did not appear, as she usually seemed to when someone had no business. He looked out again; John was gone.

Probably in search of buried treasure, Henry thought, although he had reluctantly given up his belief in that years before. Even now, however, all mysteries seemed to him rooted in buried treasure; not the gold of pirates in rural Illinois, perhaps, but maybe that of bank robbers from the Depression. Certain arrowheads were known to be priceless, and sometimes just lying on the ground, waiting. And he'd heard that people occasionally found oil in their backyards. Henry shuffled back to his room, the sunporch converted for him when mother moved to a room of her own. Peter, two years older than John, spoke in his sleep, mumbling, "Quiet." After pushing the cat out of the warm hollow she'd made in his pillow, Henry climbed in and snuggled down. There actually was wealth on the farm, he knew, horse-flesh that might sell for thousands and thousands of dollars, but it all belonged to mother. He fell into a deep sleep of prosperous dreams, in which it all belonged to him.

The scenes of the farm were not as fantastic to John as he'd hoped they would be. The barn, its neat white trim picked out by moonlight, still looked obstinately like the barn, and the nocturnal knockings of the horses within were familiar, flat, and uninteresting. He could make of the manure pile no shapes or ghouls. It looked exactly like *the* manure pile that bulked so large in his daily activities. The air, though, clear and now cool, bearing the sweet, alluring scent of clover, invigorated him, and when he rounded the corner of the orchard, the way the pasture lay thick as fur fitted his sense of what this adventure, this first night abroad, ever, should be.

The farm buildings sat on a hill embraced by the wide curve of a large creek. The two barns on one side and the white house and old orchard on the other formed a rectangle bisected by the gravel driveway. Fanning away from the central compound were fenced paddocks, stands of trees, and outbuildings for the storage of machinery. A couple housed straight stalls for horse shows and winter use. John had lived nowhere but the farm, and the nights he had spent away, at horse shows or with relatives, were so few that each remained discrete and pristine in his memory. Visits to cousins, one family in Cleveland and the other in Baltimore, had been arrestingly exotic: lawns instead of fields, afternoons among teeming strangers at giant public swimming pools, late nights of jokes, giggles, and the danger of lighting matches under the bedclothes. Once, with his cousin Fred, he had sneaked out the bedroom window, then tiptoed around the house to spy on the grownups. Most exotic of all, there had been no horses.

An undulating apron of ground spread green-black and silver to the woods below. Mares and foals, feeling safety in the peace of the weather, were scattered over the lower third of the hillside, lying down or resting in the hammocks of their own joints. From where John stood, they all looked black, but when a head turned or a leg moved, bright white floated on the moonlight. This was more like it. The idea of night rambles about the farm had seemed spectacularly deviant to him, as if his daily resentments gestated something criminal, but now, actually out here, with his body clattering inside his clothes and his quietest cough like slamming doors, he felt delightfully orphaned and mute, about to discover something, anything, even though there was nothing he didn't know already about the farm.

He stepped through dew and cottony dandelions, slid his fingers along moist fenceboards. For a moment he lay down, first with his nose against the soil, then on his back, flat, as if the sky were a stone that pressed him down. Even with the moon at half, there were stars and stars. He thought of Buddy, a rather pretentious older cousin who'd once had a telescope and set about looking for all the constellations in the northern summer sky. A telescope, a flashlight, and a star map. Buddy was very methodical. John narrowed his eyes and the moon receded, making of the night sky a tunnel pricked with diamonds. He veered toward sleep, shook his head, and stood up.

He came to the creek, where he had learned to swim (five

strokes, walk across the gravel bar, seven more strokes, turn around). Every summer the four children exhausted its possibilities by the last weeks of school, but now, as John stood on the slippery bank, drawn there by the dappling of light through the trees, he drew in his breath, as if something were about to happen. By day you could see the gravel streambed through two or three feet of clear water. Water spiders skated and dragonflies hovered and minnows skittered in your peripheral vision. By night (off to his left, and then to his right, bullfrogs splashed into the water) the pool was black; he could not see at all, but this betokened everything rather than nothing. He squatted down and stuck his hand in, half expecting to pull out a dripping wad of life itself. The water was cold and fine, delicious to his skin. John laughed aloud and at once forgave the farm for being so familiar. Anything seemed possible at night. In the water at his feet, for example, he sensed not just minnows and frogs, but bass and trout and crawdads and river clams and water snakes (he stepped back). In the woods surrounding there were surely mice, rabbits, and moles, but why not woodchucks and badgers, opossums and raccoons, even deer? Among the leafy limbs and hollows of the trees (boxelder, white ash, sugar maple, walnut, white and red and pin oak, elm and hickory, sycamore and poplar) there must be orioles and woodpeckers and bluebirds and jays and cardinals as well as sparrows, wrens, and robins. Owls and bats would be gazing upon him right this very moment. He paused, listening, and shivered blissfully. For an instant he could see it all, the densely inhabited earth and the thick stars, ready and waiting to be catalogued.

Often he yearned for other boys, the sort of mysterious other boys that his mother and probably his father would not approve of, who would follow him, but also answer his questions. Nighttime boys. His brothers were too young and too old. And too well-known. They would balk at his leadership with the blindness of blood kinship, even though it was he who had recently dilated, like the pupil of an eye, in order to see everything. It was better to be alone, though. He imagined himself with the science teacher on the first day of school (he, unlike the rest of the family, loved school), jars arrayed before them, himself modest, rather silent, the science teacher awed and garrulous. Mary Louise O'Connor would be sitting in the first row, shy but admiring, dark and trembly voiced, but certainly admiring, as he described the clever and occasionally perilous ways in which he had secured so many and such rare specimens. The science teacher would encourage him to be a biologist. Mary Louise O'Connor would simply encourage him. Ah. He could imagine never sleeping again, instead reveling nightly in his own memories and plans. All at once he seemed to himself so full that with the simple resource of thought he would never be bored again.

He followed the creek to the lower end of the gelding pasture and climbed the fence corner. He imagined himself doing this every night, doubling his life, sharpening his night vision. There would be so many nights. He trudged up the path, speaking softly as he passed among the quiet geldings, sometimes putting his hand on a rump or a shoulder, as he had been trained to do, so that he wouldn't startle a timid or sleeping equine. It was a long grassy slope, slightly dished, loud with the sawing of insects and cool with dew. He untied the gate, lifted it so that it wouldn't scrape, tied it again. Between the house and the barn were the cars.

All day there was somebody or other around the cars, precluding experimentation. Father drove an old Pontiac that didn't interest John, but mother's Datsun, small, yellow, fairly new, he thought the perfect personal vehicle. He hesitated, then opened the driver's door tenderly and sat down in the car. After a moment, he let out the parking brake. The Datsun, in neutral, rolled backward about five feet, down the gentle incline beside the barn where it was parked. A boy at school, Tommy Murphy (lately known as Tom), was reputed to have rolled his family's Mercury silently down his driveway, and then, out of earshot of the house, to have driven away four times, and once a hundred miles, to St. Louis. The keys were in the ignition, but John didn't touch them. Mother's amber crystal key bob swung with the movement of the car, then turned slowly, reflecting the pale light. John pushed out the clutch and tried shifting: first, second, third, fourth, then he engaged the parking brake again. At night no one was ever around the cars. He smiled.

The sleeping house was warmer than the outdoors, as if filled with breath. Jeepers, the Border collie, stood up to greet him when he stepped through the door, but at once curled up on the boot pile again. Floorboards creaked. The kitchen linoleum under his bare feet rasped with grit, but he made it to the stairs, then to the second floor. Only Henry's room stood between him and his bed. He peered in. Half uncovered, pressing his pillow to his side, Henry snored pacifically. John grinned, safe as safe could be.

By 7 A.M. Axel Karlson was standing in the middle of his neighbor Harold Miller's soybean field. He would never have told anyone, but the thing he liked best about the acreage, which he was about to buy, was the view it afforded of his family compound. What he liked least (the long road frontage that would demand impregnable fences and constant inspection) was entirely outweighed by this feature, although Axel would enjoy the perspective not more than once a year. Once in five, he thought, would be enough if the perspective was his own. It was for this luxury that he, an abstemious man whose loafers were resoled every other year and whose best suit still had shaped shoulders, worked ten hours a day, six days a week. With forty horses and the land to support them, plus four children and the insurance to secure them, all of his generous salary was consumed, and, periodically, principal drained off his investments.

He was not, he supposed, a man in control of his own life, and yet, straddling one of Miller's soybean rows, he was grinning.

Most of the time Axel felt as though his eyes were windows and he himself a little boy jumping up to see out of them. He had the full battery and more of adult accomplishments: a vice-presidency in a small company brought him prestige; he was sufficiently educated, and to some degree knowledgeable about literature, music, and sports; in any discussion of politics or farming, two of his primary interests, his thoughtful opinions flowed forth in grownup, masculine, self-assured tones. Miller no doubt considered him not just an opponent equal to himself, but perhaps somewhat hard, a sharp bargainer (as befitted a gentleman farmer who planted hay for many expensive horses and didn't have to watch the hog market). Axel and his wife were middle-aged, experienced adults, yet his mental image of the two of them had not changed in the two decades of their marriage: a boy in gray kneepants and a girl in an organdy party dress, holding hands in front of a big oak door, each with a handsomely wrapped birthday present and the expectation of cake, candy, and the pop of balloons.

As a matter of fact, though they no longer shared anything, what with his failed interest in the horses and her fourteen-year-old conversion to Catholicism, it was in this image that he continued to love his wife. Expectation was as tangible in her still as on the day they'd met, in a crowded elevator at Saks Fifth Avenue in New York. She was talking to a friend in her lovely, ever lovely contralto. He'd stumbled and stepped on her foot. "Excuse me," he'd said, and she had turned to him, uttering one eager syllable, "Yes?"

She had not yet come out of the house, though the children could be seen going from barn to barn, but he imagined her among them, always being called or needed or queried. Axel loved her ubiquity. Every object in their establishment was marked with some form of her name: Kate Karlson, K. M. K.,

Mrs. A. O. Karlson, Katie McGinnis, my book. A letter addressed to him was an oddity, almost a subject of resentment on her part. "Well!" she would say. "This one's for your father!" and sometimes, when the handwriting was very mysterious, he would tell her to open it, feeling much more pleasure in her interest than interest in the letter itself.

Axel bent down and broke off one of Miller's crisp and extremely green leaves. "Hello," he said to her invisible presence in the distant compound. "I have plans for you." None of his plans ever worked out, of course, and yet he was a happy man, stupidly happy, he often thought, and had been for years. He was a giant who paced an unending circle about his little farm, viewing it from every angle in all weathers, and he was a little boy, who, whenever he did catch a glimpse out of those six-foot windows, could hardly believe what he saw.

Peter Karlson was too tall, and though about to be a senior in high school, growing taller. He managed to forget this in excitement as he hung the saddle over his new mount's stall door, but he remembered it again when he returned with the bridle to find his saddle (a Stuebben much bedizened with suède) down in the dirt. MacDougal, fifteen years old himself, appeared to have his own opinions about saddles as about much else.

No one had ridden MacDougal in about two years, so Peter approached the horse crooning, the saddle on his arm. MacDougal laid his perfectly formed black ears against his skull and pulled against Peter's quick grip on the halter. Peter followed easily, still crooning, smiling. MacDougal switched his tail, pretending he was about to kick, but then began to back around the roomy stall instead, easily avoiding water buckets and feed pan, dragging Peter's shined brown boots through the customary defecation spot. It was an effective evasion, this backing in circles, because Peter could not jerk the horse's head to one side and throw him off balance. John paused in the aisle with his own mount, already tacked up. Freeway was the other truly beautiful horse on the farm, a chestnut Thoroughbred of mother's own breeding who had turned out, unlike most of mother's horses, to be fairly tall as well as solid-boned. He had been bred for John and was the only animal on the place that John was fond of. "Go away," said Peter. "An audience just encourages him."

"Life itself encourages him." John puffed his chest in mock pomposity.

"Yeah, well . . ."

"You shouldn't let her make you . . ."

"She's not making me; I asked her."

"Then you're the one who's crazy."

"He's got to be ridden."

"So you say." John strolled away; Freeway, gleaming and docile, strolled too. He looked to Peter like the incarnation of pleasure and success.

MacDougal hesitated. Peter sprang at the horse with speed born of long practice, and tossed the saddle over him. At once MacDougal became immobile, until Peter tried to tighten the girth, whereupon the horse leaned on him, pressing him against the stall door. Peter unlatched it and led him into the morning sunlight. MacDougal, having outwitted himself, now took the bit cooperatively. Feeling no triumph, Peter did not smile; this, like all Peter's victories, was diluted by growth, the tragedy of his life. Even as he mounted, he knew that in equestrian skill and tact he had just grown into mother's favorite horse, but in size he had already grown out of him. He lengthened his stirrups. They dangled below the horse's belly. Peter sighed.

It was almost eight; mother was about to appear. The Karlson children and the other students, all girls, were hurrying to mount or to warm up in the ring beside the barn. Their horses shone in the bright air, manes and tails feathery with combing, hocks and bellies brushed more than assiduously by riders who were themselves properly capped and booted, wearing crisp shirts and striped belts. One knew without looking that all tack was well soaped and all strap ends neatly confined in keepers. The horses passed and repassed one another, beautiful thin-skinned equines in rich shades of mahogany and brown. There was not much chatter. Were one's heels sufficiently down? Was the chin thrust forward again, the shoulders hunched? One or two equestrians gyrated their lower backs, striving to attain, in the next minute or so, that special elusive fluidity. Mother was about to appear; in fact, with a slam of the screen door, here she came.

Henry, the only rider without the inward look of self-perusal, slumped in the saddle, his left leg thrown casually over the pommel, tickling Mr. Sandman's ear tips with his crop. He was about to give up the whole glittering matinal cotillion. Henry saw in oats and sweetfeed roasts that he would never enjoy, and in hay bales, baked potatoes with sour cream eternally unconsumed. He knew the probable value of every animal and vegetable on the farm. He never joined in the cherry fight that annually denuded the three producing cherry trees, and his favorite fantasy was that of selling every board and bale they owned. Or rather, that mother owned. Henry was very exact about ownership. He perceived in the pastorale about him waste, only waste, and this summer he intended to give it up. Meanwhile, mother came up behind him and jabbed her clipboard into the small of his back. Henry did not lose his balance, but simply swung his leg over, found the stirrup, and trotted away. Kate Karlson thought her habitual thought: that with a little discipline he would be the best of them all.

"The horse," said Kate when her students were drawn up in a line, "is always falling down and catching himself at the last moment. He is a delicate animal for whom it is difficult to carry, push, or pull weight. Having a rider makes it more likely that, when the horse begins to fall, he will not be able to catch himself, and when the rider rides badly, the horse is subject to frequent little strains. A tendon here, a joint there, a blood vessel somewhere else, all these things are overexerted and injured when a rider leans to one side, or slumps, Henry, or presses the animal beyond the exercise good for him."

It was obvious that Peter's height came from his mother, a brisk brown woman with the soldierly posture of self-confidence. Katherine Karlson looked both older and younger than her forty-two years, because of her skin, which was ridged and freckled by the sun, and her eyes, which were bright blue and undefeated, perhaps untouched, by the pain of four difficult childbirths, a six-month tangle with tuberculosis, and a thrice-broken left arm (broken by MacDougal all three times).

She went on (as usual, thought John): "If I were to go up to this horse," she stepped up to her daughter Margaret's bay Anglo-Arab, "and push him here in the withers with one finger," she did so, "he would stumble." Herbie caught himself and jangled his bit in surprise. "Ellen." Kate turned to one of the lesson girls. "What would happen to your viola if you unwound all the strings at one time and then tuned them all up together?"

"I guess it wouldn't be very good."

"Would you do it?"

"Oh no, ma'am."

"Well, a horse is a more delicate instrument than the very best viola. His back heels are tuned to his lower jaw, his tail bone is tuned to the tips of his ears. He is alive! Alive! Everything is connected!" She beamed. "You, my dear children, distort and interrupt the connections by merely sitting there, let alone trying to ride." She looked them over, feeling pleasingly stern and sternly pleased. A group of modest talents stood before her, some of them awkward, but all of them neat and ready, devoted.

"Horses in the wild," she continued (John coughed), "are lazy, like people, and they only use the muscles they have to. They

11

have more, many more muscles, with which they can do many more things than a horse by himself would ever think of. Beautiful, graceful things! This is what riders are for, because in training a horse to carry him safely and soundly a rider can also train a horse to use his body like a gymnast.

"Today we begin the extended trot."

Actually, they had begun the extended trot numerous times in previous years. Every horse was fully trained, if not entirely willing, to lower his croup, engage his back legs, and charge forward, his fore fetlocks snapping and his lower jaw working against the bit, but Kate rather liked ritual methods of reminding her children and her students that summer vacation, which was just beginning, meant the hardest work of all.

Dear Lord, she thought as she walked behind the ten horses filing to the training field, please protect and preserve my eldest boy, and give him the tact he needs to ride my horse without getting hurt or hurting others. Even she herself had not always possessed the tact necessary to ride MacDougal, and doubted if anyone she'd known was that infallible. Since Easter, the occasion of a rash half promise that Peter could try the horse over the summer, she had prayed about and pondered the idea. Now he seemed to be doing moderately well. It was, in fact, a tribute to his agility or luck that the horse was saddled at all on the first day, much less mounted.

MacDougal: the most beautiful two-year-old Kate had ever seen when she bought him, a toast-colored bay with black stockings above the knees, a long silky tail, and haunches that even then had promised five-foot fences with six-foot spreads. She had underestimated. Sometime during Henry's second year and MacDougal's sixth, when Axel and she were still sharing secret plots, they had gone out one dawn and put the horse over a five-and-a-half-foot course ending in a six-three oxer with a spread of seven, if you included the water, which he did not touch, even with the twinkling tip of his back toe.

Kate set up her folding chair on the grassy and fragrant Irish Bank, as yet untrampled by slithering hooves. The line of students circled her untidily, bunching, then straggling apart, horses jerking the reins out of their riders' fingers, relaxing into lazy ambling, side-stepping, or throwing their heads. Although she pretended to be watching everyone (her admonitions about spacing, after twenty years, flowed ceaselessly), really she was watching only MacDougal and hoping to tire him with extended trot, an exercise he did not especially mind. Miraculously, he was moving forward, and Peter seemed relaxed, light-handed, and alert.

Once a United States Equestrian Team rider had asked to borrow the horse, and, flattered, Kate had let him. They had done a sinuous, nearly perfect collected trot into the dressage ring, and had pulled up in an absolutely square halt before the judge. The rider, a flamboyant Californian, swept off his cap and made a deep bow, not realizing that MacDougal was unaccustomed to men, and therefore to a preliminary hats-off salute. When given the signal to canter away, MacDougal had ignored it, maintaining his square, proud halt, a most beautiful horse among many beautiful horses. Again the signal, still immobility, and again the signal, this time with the minutest shadow of exasperation on the part of the foolish horseman. Kate closed her eyes. According to Axel, the man flicked his whip, the horse flicked his tail, the man applied his spurs, the horse twitched his ears, and then both exploded into the air. Three wrenching bucks brought them back to the gate, where Mac simply lay down. In front of the entire audience, Kate had had to remove all his tack and lure him to his stubborn feet with not just oats but sweetfeed and apples. The member of the Team had never spoken to her again.

She shouted, "Walk, please!" and Peter eased him down, almost successfully, although he laid back his ears momentarily and gave one annoyed little buck. Peter glanced at her. She nodded. One by one, the other riders considered, and then, with painful slowness, produced the series of movements that would bring about a walk. How far even the best of them were outstripped by Kate's vision of what they should be! Even MacDougal was out of shape and out of practice, reluctant and bumpy in his gaits, resistance tightening his whole body. And yet he knew everything. More than once in the old days she had finished a workout on him with tears on her cheeks from the perfect joy of it. He was a genius and she loved him.

"Let them relax!" Peter loosened his reins too suddenly, with too much relief. MacDougal gave a grunt, and Kate was about to speak, but then the horse dropped his head and chomped his bit, content for a moment. "Thank you, Lord," whispered Kate.

Margaret was on course. Only the hay bales, then the little brush, the crossbar (which she took very neatly), and the stone wall, but when she had finished even so brief a performance, she found Kate's eyes turning perfunctorily back to her from Peter. Kate did not look at her precisely in the way she had never not looked at her before her embarrassing return from college after just one semester. "O.K.," she said, a phrase and an abdication from criticism that Margaret had rarely heard before this last spring. Margaret nodded and took her place with the other riders. Her mother's indifference had settled over her like a plastic bubble, and its effect was unexpected. Suddenly (at last?) she and her horse were alone. Even in the smallest classes, the difficulties and pleasures of small circles to the left or two-tracks from A to K were of consequence only to them. It was lovely. It was relaxing. She forgave Herbie his occasional impatience. When she walloped him with her whip at a refusal, she did so out of benevolence, not anger. Gallops around the outside course, over the lip of the home field and under the verge of the woods, seemed like vacations. She allowed him the infrequent leaf, pulled for him an occasional handful of grass, and though she was too old and too experienced for equine infatuations, she imagined friendship between them.

Letting go the stirrups and giving Herbie the whole length of the reins, Margaret allowed herself a wide uncovered yawn and restrained stretch. Mother was urging one of the Pony Clubbers not to lean into her turns, shouting lurid descriptions of horses falling over and breaking their knees. It was mother's favorite nit for picking, and the repetition lulled Margaret pleasantly. She felt that she could go on for a lifetime of summer days, listening to mother dispense information in her precise, peculiar, redundant way. When Herbie put his nose down to snuffle the grass, Margaret was visited with the sudden odor of camomile and something else, summer savory, perhaps, and then with nostalgia for previous summers, when the treasury of odors and repetitions, of herself and her brothers just beginning and still enthusiastic, had not been broken into. The coziness of summer was what she had missed at college, and what she was looking forward to now.

One year all their mounts had been ponies, and every day mother had helped them trot over a grid of poles on the long side of the barn ring. Henry's pony was on the lead line, and Henry was instructed to hold tight, then praised lavishly after the pony hopped the final foot-high jump. Each summer they had formed a tight knot of a group, each one visible to all the others almost every hour of the day. There was a good deal of chatter, frequent bumping into one another, and much teasing and fighting. In her yellow dormitory room at college, with her roommate gone to the library or out on a date, Margaret had cried and longed to get back into the knot, and now here she was, in spite of mother's indifference, closely looped about and held. Mother informed the Pony Club girl that she was riding like a bowl of spaghetti, and tears sprang into Margaret's eyes.

"All right!" began Kate. "Assume a single-file line, Peter in the lead. . . ." And the accident befell John. He had turned to speak

15

to one of the girls, throwing his horse off balance, and the horse stepped into a hole. John tumbled off onto his helmeted head, and Freeway bobbed and halted, holding his leg off the ground in pain. Kate ordered immediate hosing with plenty of cold water, and pretended unconcern, but as always with accidents of whatever nature, the lesson was ruined. "Trot!" she snapped. "Serpentines across the hillside, down and back, four times!" When he thought he was out of her sight, John yanked the horse angrily in the mouth. Kate bit her lip.

"Margaret's bawling again," said Henry, seated at the kitchen table.

She had set the milk on the table for lunch and found the paper napkins, then Margaret felt tears coming again and ran into the bathroom. They were by no means uncommon, in fact had been daily of late: inconvenient, embarrassing, inexplicable. They'd begun at college, but hadn't ended upon her return. She had good days and bad, all of them with periods in the downstairs bathroom, a towel in one hand and a blurry *Catholic Digest* in the other (reading seemed as though it ought to distract her, but never did). Once in a while she looked in the mirror and tried to penetrate whatever it was that made not just each member of her family and every living thing on the farm so poignant (she'd wept four times at the blossoming apple trees alone) but also the gallons of milk, the pile of boots and shoes by the back door, the pictures on the walls, and the matched wing chairs in the living room, to name a few of her recent crises. Mother was wonderful about it, and said nothing. The boys too: if Henry announced to everyone that Margaret was bawling again, John usually told him to shut up. Thoughts of their goodness stole all control from her, and she sat on the sink counter, trying to muffle this abandoned boohooing in two towels and the shower curtain. She felt not happy or sad, but fleeting.

16

"Shut up." John poured milk down the side of his cereal bowl so that it ran under his Cheerios and lifted them up.

"Huh?" said Peter.

"I said, 'Margaret's bawling again.' " Henry repeated himself only out of his tragic distaste for the foodstuffs before him (Cheerios, cornflakes, Lucky Charms, Wonder bread, nameless cheap cookies, and milk).

"And I said, 'Shut up,' " remarked John, to whom this lunch was as good as any other.

"Oh." Peter threw the boot he'd just pulled off into the corner and disappeared toward the living room without bothering to eat at all.

Henry chose cornflakes. "They're both getting weird," he said. "Weird, weird, weird."

"No weirder than you, bean brain."

"Duck face." More than anything, Henry wanted to know what John had been up to the night before, but John's face fell into a scowl as he spooned up the last of the milk in his bowl, so Henry said, "You'd think she'd dry up."

"You dry up."

"Hey," said Henry.

"What do you want?"

"I got up last night to get a drink of water."

John's eyelids fluttered, but he didn't raise his glance from the funny papers he had taken up. "So what?" Henry poured milk over his cereal, afraid suddenly to ask any questions. "So what?" repeated John, now looking at his brother, his chin thrust out, and his voice edged.

"Nothing," said Henry.

John stood up.

Henry said, "Frog scrotum," and giggled at his brother's wished-for smile. John smacked the top of Henry's head. "One mortal sin," he announced. "I fine you ten Our Fathers and the Spaghettisburg Address." Unconsciously, they both looked toward the back door. Mother did not come in, however.

"Four more than eleven steers afloat," recited Henry. John had made up the words years before.

"Our fathers sought Fords upon this continent."

"A one-car nation." He leaned back in his chair and peered at his brother, who was, thank heaven, smiling as he put on his boots. When John went out, Henry turned back to his cornflakes. Soggy already. While he was dumping them into the garbage can, Peter came in, saying, "Think of the Chinese." He mimicked mother's voice perfectly.

"The Chinese are weird."

"No weirder than you, bean brain." This he said in John's voice, then he reached for the cookies.

The sun shining on them as they glanced at her would have flooded Margaret again had she not been exhausted. It almost annoyed her. After all these years, why did she have to rejoice in Peter's arched eyebrows and planed cheeks? Why did she have to see so clearly Henry's thick hair and his eyelashes that lifted like velvet curtains on a stage? They were only her brothers. "What a mess," she said aloud, referring to the kitchen.

Henry looked for the family bicycle that afternoon, and there was no transgression in it, though there seemed to be. Each of the children had flirted with the old one-speed, but each in turn had decided that a self-propelled machine without personality was nothing compared to the mysteries of a living horse. So the bicycle came to Henry, who wheeled it out of the garage and wiped it off. The decision to him was hardly as clear, although the driveway was the only place to ride.

Unpaved, it was nearly a mile long, curving away from the house in a wide S between two pastures, then dropping through thick woods to a small creek. The hill from there to the main road was the terror of all haulers of horse trailers who exhibited in the summer horse show. In consideration of the more timid,

Axel had built a row of standing stalls in the shade of two boxelders beside the entrance. Here Henry rested after his first arduous climb, tired already from the incline, the heat, and the deep gravel.

He returned to the house and started again. It was very simple. First he sat back on the seat for a quarter of a mile, pedaling steadily and holding the front wheel in a rut. Around the waves of the S he shifted his weight slightly from side to side. He watched his knees and feet rising and falling, usually driving the pedals, but sometimes propelled by them, and he watched the staccato fenceposts and the easygoing Thoroughbreds in their pastures, strolling from knoll to knoll. Starlings and bluejays perched on the fence, and a red-winged blackbird rose out of her nest at his passage, squawking and feinting toward him. At the edge of the woods he pedaled for a second or two, then the road fell steeply, so he leaned forward, steering hard and pretending not to be afraid. He aimed for the bridge. There was the exciting possibility, which came to seem with each second a probability, that he would miss it, crash into one concrete abutment or the other, smash the bicycle, and kill himself. He did not, however, press the foot brake. Instead, he lifted his feet clear of the spinning pedals and shot through, frozen and senseless; the toil up the far slope, with its frustrating drag of gravel and dirt, was mitigated by relief and exhilaration. The bike slowed, Henry's legs shook. He gave up and walked the rest of the way, promising himself as if he were grown up that the day he pedaled to the top he would ride off down the road and never return.

The vet came before dinner. He checked the two pregnant mares and declared that either of them could deliver at any time, then he had John bring Freeway out of his stall, although the beautiful chestnut could barely walk. He felt for heat and swelling in the shoulder, the elbow, the knee, the ankle, the foot. He set up his portable x-ray machine, thinking resignedly that it

19

would be years before he would see payment for this expensive bit of diagnosis, and told John to stand back. John stood back, quiet, anxious, resentful. The machine buzzed. Freeway lowered his head, taking weight off his leg. The vet packed up his machine, then felt the knee and ankle again, probing with his finger between the tendons and the bone. "Keep hosing," he said, "and tell your mother I'll call in the morning."

"It won't be worth it if I can't ride him this summer."

"Don't hold your breath."

John stuck the horse in his stall without looking at him or speaking to him, and went in to supper. It was open-faced grilled cheese, and mother had forgotten to toast the bottoms again.

ELLEN Eisen's father, who knew nothing of horses, came to Kate the next morning and made an offer for Spanky. Ellen was elated and ashamed. "This is him, daddy," she said, shyly patting the neck that, by herself, she would have embraced. Mr. Eisen cleared his throat repeatedly, embarrassed by Ellen's needs and his own, too formal, "country" clothes. He was about to spend lots of money on a mystery.

He had met Kate once or twice, and when he was shown into the shabbily elegant living room to talk about finances, he found himself at ease. Kate was brown and frank: Mr. Eisen perceived her stiffened arm as reassuring human fallibility and not a sign of the danger he was purchasing for his daughter. How courteous and comradely Kate was, and though he might have mistrusted courtesy and camaraderie over a board table, Mr.

Eisen believed in Kate. "Just a moment," she said, smiling brightly. She went to the sliding glass door, opened it, and shouted, "I said that Peter was to drive the tractor, and you know better!" Her voice, never shrill, deepened and carried commandingly. Outside, the tractor came to a halt. One boy (Mr. Eisen didn't know them apart) got down and another got into the seat. But Kate was smiling at him, recalling his attention to herself. In a maelstrom of snaffles, dandy brushes, overreaching boots, running martingales, and expense, he was glad to give it.

"Spanky is a lovely horse," she said. "I trained him myself." On the whole, Kate did not feel that she cheated these men. The horses she sold were worth but a few hundred dollars less than she charged. Certainly they were sound and well trained, and these fathers paid not just for the horses but for the reliability they found in Kate herself and the safety of her equestrian theories. You had only to look around the room to note the impeccable taste of her well-bred establishment, where one found the ambiance of Maryland, and no worrisome male stablehands. "And Ellen has been doing quite well on him. I wouldn't be surprised if a few ribbons came her way." Ellen smiled, as she was expected to, and then regarded the loop of her whip very intently. She did not want Spanky for mere ribbons. She wanted him because she loved him. Kate quoted a sum. Her voice was precise and mellifluous, so that there would be no confusion about numbers or decimal points. The father repeated the sum, and the daughter, hearing a polite doubtful tone she knew well, and also hearing a figure a good deal larger than the one she had proposed as an estimate at the dinner table, sat up in her chair, but was unable to look at her father. More clarification was unnecessary. Here was an expenditure that could not fail to bob to the surface in family disagreements. The aftertones of Kate's voice reverberated perfectly between father and daughter, and Ellen pursed her lips. To persist in her desire

22

now took courage. "Well," said Mr. Eisen, "I suppose we've gone too far to turn back, haven't we, Ellen?"

Ellen shrugged.

"Ellen is very fond of Spanky, I know," said Kate.

"I'm sure she is," said Mr. Eisen. "Why don't I speak to Ellen's mother about it and give you a call?" Promises about room cleaning and dishwashing would be exacted.

Kate nodded. "Of course. Perfectly all right." She fished in the coffee-table drawer for a business card and considered the sum of money. It was enough for Spanky, but not enough for the farm.

No matter how many fathers there were, the sums were never enough for the farm. Although Axel contributed his salary and the dividends of his investments, although there was a monthly revenue from students and a few equine boarders, and though Kate had a minuscule annual income, there was never enough for the upkeep of more than forty horses, four children, two adults, numerous large and small pieces of machinery, five buildings, miles of fencing, and three hundred acres of topsoil. Gates were tied shut with baling twine. Clothing, always bought on sale, passed, whether it fit or not, from one child to the next. With the veterinarian there was a standing debt, as well as with the blacksmith, and the children had more than once been told that rice pudding, if made with plenty of milk and raisins and sweetened with brown sugar, was nutritious enough for anyone's dinner. Kate, whose conviction of her own business acumen was lifelong, marveled that other, more poorly guided families could afford anything at all in these times of expense and inflation.

"Let me offer you some coffee, or better still, iced tea," she said. She led Mr. Eisen and Ellen into the kitchen. While they were sitting at the table, a number of boys, who Mr. Eisen assumed were her sons, tramped through. One stopped for milk at the refrigerator. Another, the tallest, was handsome, and resembled Kate, until you looked back again and saw that something indefinable in her created something missing in him. Her skin and hair were dry and uncared for, but her eyes had the glittery, splintery look of shattered mirrors. She was talking. Somehow, they had gotten onto the subject of miracles. Ellen fidgeted. Mr. Eisen sent her out, then said, "Excuse me, I didn't hear you?"

Kate nodded cordially. "I was telling you about the miracle I was party to a few years ago. Longer than a few, actually." She smiled beatifically upon the boy at the refrigerator, who scowled and stomped after the others. "When John was born I was told that I simply had to walk every day for at least an hour. The birth, you see, was especially difficult, and my doctor was of the active rather than the invalid school." Mr. Eisen could hear a voice in the living room say, "Here we go again. You'd think I was to blame for the whole thing."

Kate was continuing. "There was a lovely mare boarding here at the time, a pet, actually, of a friend of mine, who had been a splendid event horse, but was foundered. Founder is a disease of the laminae inside the horny part of the horse's hoof. They swell against the shell of the hoof and cause the horse a lot of pain. I wanted Mildred to put the horse down, which is, of course, what is done with most foundered animals." Mr. Eisen blanched, thinking of such a profitless end to such a large investment. "It's purely a matter of carelessness, and no horse living on this place has ever foundered. Anyway, this mare was turned out with the broodstock in the far pasture, and I would walk there, rain or shine, every day, because I liked to check the horses, and it took exactly an hour."

"She's still at it!" exclaimed the voice from the living room, and the door slammed.

Kate appeared not to have noticed. "I begged and begged Mildred to have the horse destroyed. The poor thing was in

24

tremendous pain. One day (I was thinking about this the day before yesterday because it was just about this time of year) I was taking my walk in the rain. I got caught in that pasture when a sudden thunderstorm came up, and I was standing in a hollow near an old outbuilding, watching the mares. Mildred's horse was off by herself a ways, by the fence. Often an injured animal will be excluded from the group, especially in any sort of crisis, even the crisis of a thunderstorm." Mr. Eisen nodded, as if this was a bit of homely wisdom that could be applied in many circumstances, but actually he was thinking how profound this silly story sounded floating in the liquid of Kate's voice. "And then, just when I was thinking about John and how mad he would be if I missed his feeding, because I've always breastfed well into the second year, and he was the most demanding of all" (there was a thump and a cry from the living room) "there came an incredible boom and flash, and the mare was struck down, the fencepost beside her was scorched, and all the broodstock began galloping toward the woods. Killed! Right before my eyes. It seemed like a miracle to me, it really did. God spoke to me about the proper kindness to animals, and I felt it. Well, and this is really true, when I got back to the house, there was of all things a priest at the door, with some story about his car and a puddle, and we got to talking, and it changed my life."

An obscure ardor made itself felt inside Herbert Eisen, and though he didn't for a moment believe in the miraculous nature of this event, he found himself vividly noticing Kate's white teeth and bony shoulders and strangely bent arm. "How fascinating!" he said, and thought that he sounded convincing. Kate was shaking her head in fifteen-year-old wonder. "Oh dear," she said, "the children say that I embarrass them with these stories, but a miracle is a miracle, isn't it?" Mr. Eisen nodded. "Bless you," she went on, and suddenly he knew that, if she did believe in the children's embarrassment, it would mean nothing to her. A very interesting woman, he thought, full of integrity. And

25

something else too (he looked at her eyes again) but something he could not define.

The argument ranged throughout the house. He pursued her from the dinner table, asserting, "I won't. I won't. I won't." When she went into the bathroom, he stood outside shouting "No!" and she was forced to be autocratic when she wanted to be alone. And then, when she caved in to the indignity of saying something through the door, he replied, "I can't hear you!"

The subject was a horse named Teddy that Kate wished John to ride in place of Freeway. Teddy, otherwise known as The Train, was one of the best-coordinated and best-schooled mounts on the place. He also happened to be lazy, stubborn, and ugly. All things considered, he was the only horse capable of taking John through the summer's equestrian work—those young enough were not enough schooled, and those sufficiently developed were either already spoken for or too old. Considering the jerk she had seen John give Freeway's mouth, Kate was not dismayed by the punitive element in things as they turned out, but had she had another horse, she would certainly have considered mounting the boy otherwise. However, she didn't.

"You do!" contradicted John as she opened the bathroom door, and she was startled by the look he gave her, not a child's look at all, but the wide-open, contemptuous look of an angry adult. She realized at once, perhaps for the first time, that his eyes were of a height with hers. Then he veiled himself in customary respect, and she felt in herself the memory of this politic attitude. In the midst of the loudest contradictions of one's parent, one was careful to insert an undertone of self-doubt, of entreaty, that ceded power to the parent. "Why can't I ride Chips?" he demanded. "He needs the work. So does Treasure. You don't have to breed her this year. Half the horses on this place don't get ridden anyway. Lambert Smith said last year that we've got so much good horseflesh around here that we have to let it go because we can't take proper care of everything. I could ride Bingo or Jolly!" Recognition of herself in him did not render her any less positive that his greatest equestrian (and apparently personal) growth would result from conflict with Teddy.

"Only babies ride him! He's a beginner's horse!"

"Teddy is a horse who has been called to many positions in life. Mary Rogers rode him on the B team that went to the national rally."

"Five years ago! He's older than I am!"

"Which is old neither for horse nor man."

"He's stupid."

"Right. That's why he succeeds better than any horse on this place in doing exactly what he wants, no matter who the rider is."

"He's ugly."

"If you take blues with him, everyone will just say how cute he is."

"I won't."

"What?"

"I won't do anything! Nothing! I won't even get up tomorrow."

Knowing she had momentarily retrieved the child out of the man, Kate turned and allowed Axel to say as he walked by, "Time for bed, John."

"Agh!" John jumped at her, putting his face right next to hers and grimacing frightfully.

"Go to bed!" she yelled, and, recognizing the note of true anger in her voice, he did as he was told.

Kate was reserved with her husband, and practically never spoke to him in their nightly half hour alone together. As a rule she contemplated her own schemes. Often she read *The Chronicle of the Horse,* watching for names she knew, trying to damp down suspicion of names she didn't know, and wishing, occasionally, that she had the money and the time to send her horses out East, where the Team was, and where the proper arena for equestrian skill would always be, in spite of California and Chicago. She forgot Axel's youthful presence, except to feel ill at ease if he seemed about to jump up and prowl around. He was a man without substance to her: underweight, without religion, as ready, it seemed, to run or skip or fall down as a child. These reading projects he undertook (the latest was someone named Oscar Spangler or Spengler) were to her the emblem of his nature. Every time she happened to notice, he was beginning something new.

Tonight, however, she was somehow set in motion by the argument with John, and she wanted to speak. There was an undesired momentous quality about breaking the silence. Axel sat casually in the chintz wing chair, frosted with lamplight, his right arm arched over his head like the branch of a tree, his left hand spread across the book. While he read he made noises— little coughs or hums, and sometimes the pronunciation of a word (not always difficult ones, either; as she watched, he muttered "body"). He was as without dignity this evening as ever, and his boyishness touched her as little, though she liked his thick blond hair. Still, she wanted without preamble, without a preliminary and unnatural attraction of his attention to herself, to say, "How is it?" Suddenly she desired to know if he was enjoying his Spangler, if reading it was making any difference to him, her husband of close to twenty years.

In the pumping of her heart and the moisture of her palms she almost lost her courage. The moment from the incipient wish to the clenched stomach and trembling hands was too brief, and the occasion when she could have spoken without tuning in passed. She considered what she was going to say: "How is it?" or "How's the book?" or "What are you reading these days?" and each seemed more stilted than the last. She closed her eyes and took a deep breath.

His book smacked shut, the light switch clicked, and she opened her eyes to him vanishing up the hall stairs. "How is it?" she shouted. "How's your book?"

He returned with the delight she had so hoped to avoid. "Yes?" he said. "What?"

"Nothing."

He made an annoyed little bow. "Nothing, indeed."

Ultimately, Kate decided in bed, it was just as well not to endanger the elegant clarity of the status quo.

During the sit-trot, Teddy ran up on Herbie, who put back his ears and threatened to kick, and during the posting trot, he would not move out unless John pounded his sides. He cut all corners and flattened all circles, large and small. He would not take the proper lead at the canter, and would take mouthfuls of grass, bracing his teeth against the bit and jerking John out of the saddle. He knew the high-headed evasions, the jaw-jutting evasions, and the brute-strength evasions. He was wearing John out, both his energy and his patience, so Kate cut the first half of the class short and went on to the jumping, usually the least of evils when one was starting out with Teddy. He refused the logpile three times and John fell off. Kate handed him a sturdy whip. The fourth time Teddy went over the fence, but took off too soon and left John behind. In spite of her certainty, Kate grew almost afraid. The usual chatter among the other riders stilled, and as John trotted back up the field, his face red and full of angry hatred, Kate felt strangely disobedient. "You're doing fine . . . " she began.

"I loathe this horse. I abominate him! He shits!"

"Mary Rogers . . ."

"Damn Mary Rogers!"

"You'll get bet . . ."

"Hell!"

"John, don't . . ."

"Fuck! I said 'fuck'!"

"Say it again, please." He did not, and she could see that he was angrily afraid, having broken suddenly into new territory. Two years before Axel had thrashed Peter with a hunting crop for cursing at Margaret, and that only a "goddamn."

"Again, I said."

"Fuck." He coughed.

"Thank you. Dismount, please." Teddy yawned, then helped himself to grass. His ears flopped in perfect self-confidence, and he cocked one back hoof. Kate took the reins, but declined the crop John offered her. "Theodore, stand up!" she ordered. In a second, she was on top of him and he was describing a large circle in a nicely collected and extremely surprised trot. Two small circles to the left. Two to the right. Figure eight at the canter with a flying change of lead. Halt. Back four steps. Extended trot down the long side of the ring. Teddy's tongue dropped out of his mouth in his effort to take the bit. "Stop that," she said. His poll bent, his neck arched, and he began to sweat. She brought him down to the collected trot again, this time almost a *passage*, and made him two-track across the ring, a lovely diagonal movement with Teddy's ankles crossing one another like a dancer's. Around the end of the ring at a normal trot, then two-tracks the other way. Walk, halt. A moment's relaxation, then she picked him up again and took him over the stone wall and the rails. When she returned him panting to her son, she said, "Teddy is not a beginner's horse. If he were, I would not have mounted you on him."

For lunch Kate made them a treat: peanut-butter-and-bacon sandwiches with cucumbers and tomatoes on the side. Before they thundered in, a moment of motherhood, fathomless and self-contained, like a blue bead, was given her. She was not, just then, a failed equestrian, a bluegrass exile in soybean country, a would-be nun, an ambitious riding coach. She was not the person to whom motherhood was an eighteen-year surprise. She

30

loved them as they came in: Peter too tall, John too temperamental, Margaret too sentimental, Henry too careless. She even loved them when John dropped the plate of cookies and Henry and Peter each stepped on one before Margaret could pick them up. Out of love for them, she said, "I'm putting up a new housework schedule today, and this summer I expect you to stick with it."

In the early afternoons, when the children were outside or upstairs, Kate retreated to the living room and pulled the doors shut behind her. Even on the hottest summer days, she prized her privacy more than an occasional breeze. Ostensibly she had work to do: there were accounts to be written up and horse shows to be considered and possibly entered, items to be ordered from Kauffman's or Miller's in New York, people and businesses to be corresponded with or telephoned. Actually, though, the chores dissolved in the pleasure of her solitude, and the living room never seemed to her an arena of work, like the kitchen or the bedroom or the barns. In her mind's eye she sat there, in the domesticated golden sunlight, on the once cerulean velvet sofa, lapped around by carpets and books and mahogany, solitary and content, as if, in fact, cloistered. (She swore up and down that, had she converted before marriage, there would have been none of this horse business, none of these children.) The silver on the sideboard tarnished so slowly that it seemed merely to be fading, the stacks of horse magazines grew discreetly, and, since she and Axel never entertained, the living room took on a permanent, close-fitting privacy that centered around these two daily hours, from one to three, when the world knew by instinct to leave her alone. In the other twenty-two hours of the day, she squirreled away her more difficult problems like nuts, saving them for this time and this place, when she could take them out and luxuriate in them: if not finding solutions, then at least defining them down to almost visible dimensions.

In the early days of June, she let herself pat and poke at the problem of Margaret, which was serious enough to be interesting, but not yet desperate, since the girl herself, though tearful, seemed not unhappy. Margaret, she decided after a few days' thought, could be a teacher or a nurse, something helpful and secular, but also somewhat virginal. Later on, after a little experience, she might come to marriage and children, but a girl needed a trade, Kate felt, especially if she was not very pretty or vivacious, however kind-hearted. After thinking it out in the abstract golden living room, Kate called Margaret in for confidences.

Her daughter had grown already into one of the sort of women Kate could never get along with: emotional, large-breasted, hesitant. At one time there had been some speculation that she would become a nun. Her religious early teens had been more fervent than most, and once Kate had come upon a suitcase in Margaret's closet, leaned against the wall and spread with a white towel. To the right was Margaret's daily missal, and to the left a collection of prayers for various occasions. Above the makeshift altar and below the brass crucifix, a small gold box thumbtacked to the wall contained a rosary, and taped so as to shine down over all was the flashlight Kate had been looking for in the first place. When Kate questioned her about it, Margaret confessed to fifteen rosaries a night, unless she happened to fall asleep in the middle. Kate had praised her guardedly, and watched her in church. After a while it subsided, and Margaret started kneeling upright at the rail and looking around surreptitiously during Mass like the rest of the children. The rosary was left at home, and the lace mantilla gave way to a demure circlet. Confession ceased to be a daily event, and there was no more secret fasting. Since then, however, Kate had been unable to conquer her sense that Margaret was somehow fragile, somehow pious, and somehow rather weak. When Margaret laughed at her father's jokes (not really a rare occurrence) Kate was in the habit of being mildly surprised.

"Mother?"

"You can close the door, Margaret." Kate didn't know how to elicit confidences, or even how to make them. She lay back against the arm of the blue sofa, as if invitingly relaxed. Margaret sat upright in Axel's wing chair. The curly fringes of her hair were damp; she was everything, they both knew, that was opposed to her mother's neat coolness. Kate decided to stress teaching over nursing. "I've been thinking about you," she said. "Will you try again at college this fall?" She sensed that in avoiding sentimentality she was coming out accusatory.

Margaret shrugged. "I can if you think I should."

"Now that's just the wrong reply, Margaret. I don't think anything about it. I want to know what you want to do."

"I'm fine."

This too was the wrong reply. In spite of herself Kate grew annoyed. "Of course you're not fine." She tried to clarify her point. "There's no place here for you anymore." Margaret looked at her very suddenly and very briefly. "Of course there's always a place here. I mean that any eighteen- or nineteen-year-old worth . . ." She stopped, took a breath, and started again. "You children always say you're fine when it's patently obvious . . ." And now she was sitting up straight. She reclined carefully again. "Now, Margaret," she began, and stopped. Perhaps, she decided, since the subject was broached, it would be better to just sit quietly until Margaret herself said something. Out in the barn, John and Henry were yelling back and forth to one another. Margaret said quietly, "I am fine. I don't think the crying is all that important, really."

"I wasn't thinking of that, although, of course, it does rather disturb me that you . . ."

"I am fine, really."

"I don't understand it myself, but it seems . . ."

"Mother, you never cry. You think it's a big deal because you never do it, but it isn't."

"Well . . ." It was true that Kate had never cried in her life. Even as a baby she had screamed or shouted, but never shed tears. She had stood dry-eyed at the funerals of her father and mother, at the hunting field destruction of her first and best-loved horse, at the rabies diagnosis of her prize Golden Retriever bitch, at the whinnying screams of three trapped dressage horses in a barn fire in Pennsylvania. When the horse trailer belonging to a friend rolled, fully loaded, over an embankment, and the head and back leg of one of the horses appeared in unnatural relationship to one another, it was Kate who jimmied open the trailer door, tranquilized the animal, and dared to look at the damage. Six months later, when the friend herself fell in a horse show and had her pelvis crushed, Kate was the first into the ring with blankets and brandy. Through all her injuries and childbirths she had remained open-eyed, alert, and silent.

Now she changed the subject. "Margaret," she said, sitting up and leaning forward conspiratorially, smiling at the perfection of her own plan. "Margaret, you would make a fine teacher. You're very good with children, I think. You always do much better with the beginners than I do. I think you really have quite a knack, though you may not see it. Now I think if you had some purpose, some goal that you were working for, then this crying would stop. Perhaps it doesn't bother you, but surely you'd be better off without it?"

"Sometimes I think . . . Well, you know, mother, in the Middle Ages there was this woman named Margery Kempe, and she cried all the time. They said it was some kind of visitation from the saints. She couldn't help herself. People began to avoid her."

"Well . . ." About miracles other than her own Kate did not know quite what to say, although she kept an open mind. "But anyway, think about this teacher idea. It seems like a good one to me. Third grade, fourth grade, something like that."

"I don't want to be a teacher." In its baldness, the statement seemed rather cruel, and Kate smiled, anxious to seem unhurt. Margaret shrugged sheepishly again, rushing to seem unhurtful. After a minute, Kate said, as if idly, "Where did you hear about this Margery Kempe?"

"In my medieval history course."

"Oh."

There was another long pause.

Margaret said, "I thought I'd go out and look over the broodmares this afternoon."

"Good idea."

Margaret left. Kate heard her sigh as she closed the door behind her, and had to sigh herself.

In the way that most people cannot remember not walking Kate could not remember not riding. In Maryland families of the tradition and connections her family possessed, horseback riding was the only truly acceptable sport, and sport the only truly acceptable form of recreation. It was not known how much money they had. Mother dressed superbly, there were two servants, riding boots and breeches were custom-made, and the annual subscription to two local hunt clubs was as inevitable as nourishment, but there were complaints about extravagance, and Kate was encouraged to attend a nearby girls' college, which suited her because she didn't want to leave her horses behind anyway. She bargained for her best mounts, and bought them green and gawky. When she found out what other local riders paid for their pushbutton hunters, she was indignant for them rather than envious. From her mother and father she had imbibed manners, taste, a certain eloquence, and conversance with a modicum of culture, but it was an unconscious inheritance. She had never for a moment directed her energies toward any activity besides horses until her conversion. To begin to fathom

Margaret's condition of futurelessness was beyond her. Even if you didn't want to be a teacher, she thought, it was better to think you did until you wanted to be something else.

Margaret was happily cleaning: cleaning because the upstairs closet needed it (she actually found a pair of overalls with snapping inseams, relics of Henry's years in diapers), and happy because the huge cedar-paneled space was dark and cool as well as private. She'd been there two hours already, folding old clothes and tying up bundles for the Goodwill. It astounded her how much there was, and what a lot of it she particularly remembered, as if the sight of a dress or a plaid shirt could do away with years of other dresses and shirts. Few of the clothes had holes or patches, and a number of them were neatly folded and with sales slips tucked into the packages they had come home in, relics of mother's habit of picking up things at sales that turned out to fit none of the children. Mother would then throw them into the big closet, vowing to give them to some other child at the next birthday, and here they all were.

In addition to clothing, there were skeins of yarn and half-finished sweaters, pieces of fabric, old patterns, galoshes, boots, shoes, three fedoras, many caps for winter and summer, broken toys and tools, a set of paints, an envelope of photograph negatives, a stack of picture frames, and three sewing boxes. Margaret didn't know how to sew, and Kate hadn't made anything in years, but the sewing boxes were lovely. One, of walnut and lined in yellow silk, had belonged to her grandmother, who'd liked to make her own underwear, gossamer and richly trimmed. She'd taken all the stitches by hand. Such a finely feminine accomplishment appealed to Margaret in its very strangeness, for the only underwear practical when you were riding and doing chores and sweating all day was waist high and pure cotton. Her grandmother's elegance had been merely forbidding during Margaret's childhood, but now, spreading

36

flat and then folding up nubby yellowed lengths of lace, she sighed nostalgically, imagining the discrimination and the expertise that had gone into their choosing, and that would have gone into their use.

The door opened, and father said, "Margaret, you're in there?"

"Hi, daddy. I'm rooting out the old clothes."

"Did you find my supercap, and the Sweater of Invisibility?"

"Oh, daddy."

"Oh, daddy, what?"

Margaret smiled, but did not say anything.

"Oh, daddy, what? You're smiling. You must have found them."

"Oh, daddy, they don't exist."

"Don't think, my dear girl, that just because you've been to college and taken a semester of psychology you know everything."

"I didn't take psychology, I took chemistry."

"C six, H twelve, O six, and all that?"

"More or less."

"More? Or less?"

"Too much more, I'm afraid."

"Well, what did I tell you? You should have taken psychology."

Margaret shut the beautiful box, having ordered the spools of thread into precise rows, and then balled a multicolored tangle between her palms. Axel watched her for a second, then left and closed the door. Margaret began picking up the pieces from old games: Clue, The Game of the States, Careers. All faded but newish looking. Even in winter there had always been other things to do than play games. The door opened again. "Margaret, might you go back to college and take psychology?" said Axel.

"You've been talking to mother."

"Why? Has she been after you about this?"

"Not exactly after me."

"Will you tell me what you told her?"

"I don't want to be a teacher."

"Oh. Had you told her that you did?"

"No."

"Oh." The obvious question hung between them, but Axel did not ask it. Instead, he picked up one of the boys' old baseball caps and perched it on his head. "This might be it," he muttered theatrically, "but on the other hand, it never did much for John's baseball playing."

"Oh, daddy."

He squatted down, and tucked the baseball cap under the string of one of her parcels. "Margaret."

"Yes, sir?"

"Your mother and I certainly haven't talked about this, so I'm not reporting to you officially, but I do think it's very important, when one is your age, not to get into the habit of quitting something or failing at something. It's a very hard habit to break."

"Yes, daddy."

"That sounds like an official, no-comment-so-mind-your-own-business sort of reply."

"It isn't. I'm not in that habit."

"Well . . ."

"I'm not. I'm fine, really."

"O.K." Axel stood up. "Can I take some of these bundles down to the car for you?"

"I'd love it."

Margaret did not blame them for their concern, but neither did she share it. Since her return, the farm had seemed outside the normal grip of time, an arena of endless summer, endless exertion, endless security. Change was something she no longer quite believed in.

It grew dreadfully hot, so hot that the horses were sweating in their stalls and the geese had given up their continual foraging to settle under the lilac bushes by the house. John hosed and hosed Freeway's leg, three times a day, an hour each time, and his temper got shorter and shorter. He was hosing when Mr. Eisen came to pay for Spanky. He put down the hose and ran to get his mother. The check, he saw, was for more than he knew the horse was worth, and though he hosed calmly while they were standing there (Ellen's father grateful and apologetic, Kate benevolent), once he was left alone he had to run around behind the barn and scream at his mother's dishonesty.

The afternoon was even muggier. He turned the water over himself, but in seconds even that felt like sweat. And he was sitting in the sun because the hose wasn't long enough to reach around the corner of the barn. The sun made him feel funny, very breathless and far away from himself; when he'd hosed five minutes the braiding rivulets down Freeway's leg made him dizzy. Ten minutes seemed like half an hour, and he was nauseated to think of the fifty long ones ahead.

In the days since the accident, Freeway had come to have the droop-headed, gingerly look of a lame horse. It was more attitude than lack of conditioning. He no longer seemed, even when just walking, to be moving lightly upward and forward; instead he slouched, depressed and heavy-footed. This sudden lack of elegance robbed John of his sympathy and made the hosing a duty, so, although he was faithful about doing it and knew that once he got started it really wasn't that unpleasant or even boring, he put it off a little each day so that it loomed huge most of the time. Now, he threw down the hose in disgust and decided to hike through the broodmare pasture down to the woods, because even if the blazing walk brought a headache and the grass seed stuck itchily to his damp skin, the smooth, cool pebbles and running water would be worth it. It was almost impossible to stand. Dust and gravel, burning white fences: it all seemed endless. John felt lost in himself, with few thoughts and those like bare rooms off long corridors. Even the expectation of the stream, as he parted the high grass and Freeway limped behind him with an irritating rhythm, grew worthless and old. There were a great many things he hated, and primary among them was sunshine. He hadn't the energy to enumerate the others, but he supposed that the list would be a catalog of the world.

Left. Right. Left my wife with thirty-six children, home in the kitchen in a starving condition with no gingerbread left. Dum-dit, dum-it, dum-dit went Freeway's forelegs in the dumb dirty dust behind him. They came to a path made by the mares and foals. John paused. Freeway nudged his arm with his beautiful velvety muzzle, flared his nostrils peacefully, and pricked his ears. His coppery face was veined and intelligent. Now rocky ground and trees. Shade. Flies. A disappointment, these leaves filmed with dust, unmoving, but he could hear the creek, and then it was before him, wet and clear, mud and pebbles in paradisiacal complement, the banks glistening dark, blanketed in shade. John felt himself knit together. Freeway blew and tossed his head. They came to a declivity of the bank and the horse would go no further. "Come on!" said John, yanking the halter. "Come on!" The stream, which was shallow here, ran clear and musical in its bed. Freeway set himself against the lead rope. John yanked him to the left, then to the right, but the horse's refusal to enter the water was absolute. John broke a branch from the nearest elm and began to hit him over the head and neck, advancing as Freeway retreated. The leafy branch rose and fell, and the horse jerked and jerked at the rope in John's hand.

The branch broke and he threw it down. Freeway was bleeding over the left eye and across the nose, and when John lifted his hand to push back the horse's forelock, he threw up his head and nearly got away. Somehow, John was surprised at this, and hurt. His anger spent, he had worlds of patience now. "Get in the water, Freeway," he said. "It'll be so cool." He led the horse down to the ford, then tried to walk him upstream to the shade. Freeway balked and hesitated at every step, and when John turned toward him, he shied. "Come on, now," the boy crooned. "I won't hit you again. Really not. Cross my heart."

The horse would go no further than ankle deep, but it was enough. The water slipped around John's rubber boots, cooling his feet and calves, refreshing his blood as it flowed upward to his heart. He sank his arms in to the elbows, then splashed Freeway's leg with a gentle motion. He said, "Isn't that better? Isn't that better?"

At feeding time, the bright chestnut banged his buckets like the other horses, but when John came in with the grain, he stood in the corner and laid back his ears. This was more vivid and shocking than anything about the beating, which seemed to John to have taken place at a great distance; the sight of his horse's brown eye rolling white (the horse bred and trained just for him) made John's insides feel as if they were concentrating, heating up, draining away from his skin. After dinner he turned down a game of Crazy Eights with Henry (mother said, "You boys have saddles to soap, anyway") and went up to his room.

While they were eating, clouds had blown in from the west, and air moved through the papers on his desk, making friendly noises. The disks of the shell chimes someone had given mother on Christmas knocked together, and he could hear Freeway, Herbie, and MacDougal rummaging about in their stalls, for his windows gave onto the driveway, the barn ring, and the main barn. He could, in fact, hear everything: through the open downstairs windows, Peter and Henry were arguing over whether the pitcher was a pot or a dish, since it was between these categories that the division of washing-up labor lay.

41

Margaret was out in the driveway, slapping curry combs against a fenceboard and singing to herself. Jeepers, the border collie, barked. A cat yowled somewhere nearby, and one of the broodmares over the hill whinnied to her foal. "A pitcher is a dish," shouted mother, "and I don't want to hear any more about it."

"I told you," remarked Peter.

"It wasn't my fault," said John aloud to himself. "It was too hot."

But he started to cry, anyway, not because he had done a cruelty, and one that defied his entire equestrian upbringing, but because the new mistrust between himself and his horse was so sad.

Just then, something happened that had happened once or twice before. In the midst of the grief that he should be feeling, and actually did feel, he thought the words "So what?"; not seriously, not as if he believed them, but with the same curiosity he might experience in trying on an outrageously flowered shirt. After thinking those words, he stopped crying and sat up. Strewn tragically around him, emphasized by the piercing blue of twilight and the clarity of his own washed sight, were all his uncompleted projects: the guitar he knew six chords on, the basketball he had browbeaten out of his father last Christmas (sometime soon someone would ask, "Say, whatever happened to that basketball you thought you wanted so badly last Christmas?"), stamps and coins, rocks and dried flowers. *Genetic Determination of Coat Color in the Domestic Equine, Birds of North America, Stalking the Wild Asparagus.* A camel's hair brush, nineteen sheets of rice paper, and a book entitled *Teach Yourself Chinese, Level One.* A one-thousand-piece jigsaw puzzle, one third completed (there were pieces on the floor that should have been picked up months ago). The science fair project, on the nutritive content of alfalfa, that never got to the science fair. His division of the circumference of a circle by the diameter. He'd intended to carry pi out to a hundred figures, just to see them. He'd achieved sixteen. He started to cry again, but gladly, too gladly, as if the "so what" had offended him. He cried himself to sleep, not without thinking, "I'm crying myself to sleep."

He awoke in the same blue that was so revealing of his failures, with the same cool breeze animating his possessions. He got up to take off his clothes and realized by the swell of light outside his window and then the absence of activity downstairs that it was morning. In not more than half an hour, Margaret would be waking them and issuing reminders: "No feed for the yearlings today, vet's coming to worm. Blah. Blah."

He was not hungry, and felt drained of his usual morning self-confidence. The room lightened. John hoisted himself out of bed and went to the window. The sun was up and blazed along the whole horizon. Low clouds, like rolling smoke, hung above the conflagration, and in the glare, summer trees stood seared and leafless; the barns and fences looked black, as if charred. He knew that it was only the sunrise, and yet did not know it; knew that the vermilion smeared over his arms and no doubt face was refracted light, and yet did not know. He knew that he could take refuge in sounds: chickens, horses, bluejays, swishing tree limbs, and yet doubted it. He uttered no word, held tight to the window ledge, and waited.

The fire receded, collapsed, became the distant sun. Trees burgeoned. Fences and window trim again glittered white. The old mother cat came trotting down the driveway with a barn swallow between her jaws and the entire cataclysm gathered into the rumpled wing of a dying bird. "Everybody up," called Margaret, "fly baths today!" John pushed the hair out of his face and sighed, deciding to do as his mother told him, to be innocent and good.

THE days had fallen into their summer routine. The children were out of bed by six, mounted by eight, mounted again by ten, though more informally upon the greener, less conditioned horses. They broke for lunch at noon, cleaned stalls during the heat of the day, and rode briefly again after three-thirty. On the margins of these major activities, they were also to clean, oil, tack together, splice, glue, tie up, and find dirty, squeaky, broken, frayed, and lost equipment, as well as keep up with their individual responsibilities: Margaret inspected the horses and doctored minor injuries; Peter took care of the three stallions; John watched over the yearlings and two-year-olds; Henry fed the geese, the dog, and the cats, and hunted out chicken eggs (ideally before they'd begun to rot). There were saddles and bridles to soap, boots and breeches and blankets and buckets and feed pans to be taken care of, rooms to be cleaned, and housework to share. Mother liked tea and cinnamon toast brought to her in the morning. She also liked them to pursue their equestrian education with their minds as well as their bodies: to learn rules and theories of different styles of riding and stable management, to know something about the anatomy and nutrition and psychology of the horse, to be able to converse about the history and uses of equines generally. The relationship of Grévy's zebra and Man O' War should not be outside their ken, so she left riding books, vet books, archeological books everywhere.

On Sundays they went to Mass at a smallish country church, then came home to do all their chores except riding. On Sundays, Kate felt, one rested by redoubling one's efforts at keeping the place up and the horses well cared for. Sometimes, too, Kate used Sunday to rehash their mistakes of the previous week, advancing her opinion that if they just thought about things hard enough they would not make the same ones in the week to come.

With Peter and MacDougal, this method did not seem to be working at all. Each day, with the firmest resolutions to be calm and helpful, Kate would lose her temper and get sarcastic, and each day, with the firmest resolutions to recall everything he had learned (before she reminded him of it) Peter would climb aboard his horse and turn blank. Toward the end of every lesson the vacuum in him would fill with anger, even though he was not normally an angry person and had prayed himself to sleep the night before in an effort to avert this.

A by-product of the daily conflict, and one that Kate was not too busy to notice, was that the other students were improving slightly; more importantly, however, they were exerting themselves intently. Each one had the furtive, troubled look of a man in a sudden thunderstorm, anxious not to attract the lightning of her scorn.

It got so that everything about her eldest son offended her: his new boots that were already half an inch too short, his hair that was already half an inch too long, the stiff set of his back, the limp dangling of his legs, the way his hands, which had until now been so light and responsive, unconsciously clutched at the reins, so that MacDougal bobbed and squealed in protest. His frustration and helpless anger toward the end of every lesson annoyed her, but it was his diffidence (the way he glanced at her for continual aid and encouragement, the way he flinched at the sound of her voice) that made her want to rage at him. She took this hard nut of anger with her into her den every afternoon, but came to no conclusions. Her best child and her best horse had come together, and apparently to the destruction rather than the realization of her hopes. People from the East, from the Team, would be around this summer, and she would have nothing to show them, after all.

Outside of lesson time, Peter began doing jobs he would normally have pretended to forget. One day, he washed the cars, though casually, as if only working, not trying to please anyone. Another day he cleaned up his room without being asked, and when it was mentioned in Kate's hearing, made sure to say that he had been looking for his bootjack, although the family owned so many bootjacks that one more or less meant nothing. He cared for the three stallions assiduously, grooming them every day. Then, at breakfast one day, he volunteered to get out the tractor and shovel and clean the rows of visitors' stalls in the gelding paddock. John, who would be involved in the operation, looked up in surprise, but said nothing. He had his own virtue to establish. Kate said, "That should have been done before now," but they could tell she was taken aback. She hadn't mentioned it yet herself this summer.

It was a hot job, but not too onerous. John was to loosen the dried muck with a pitchfork, then Peter was to run the tines of the tractor shovel under it, scoop it out, and carry it to the manure pile. Each stall took about ten minutes, and there were thirty stalls. Once the whole was done each summer, it did not have to be done again, and one more huge, looming project was out of the way. Furthermore, because mother was elsewhere, watching other children, they could take lots of breaks and joke around. When they were actually out there, though, booted, gloved, and equipped, John suspected that Peter was going to be so desirous of virtue that he'd insist there be no fooling around at all. What he didn't expect was that after five stalls Peter would offer to let him drive the tractor.

"It's hot up here," he told John.

"So, it's hot everywhere." Now that the offer had been made, John was reluctant, although he loved the tractor, a '36 John Deere Axel had picked up at a farm auction.

"Don't you want to?"

"Yeah, I want to."

"Well, then."

"She'll kill me."

"I'll tell her I got you to."

"She'll kill you."

"You're fifteen. You ought to be practicing. Anyway, she'll never know."

"O.K." He drew his agreement out doubtfully, as if preparing for an I-told-you-so, but once atop the machine he couldn't help twisting around on the seat in his elation and bouncing up and down.

"Watch what you're doing."

"Yeah, yeah."

"O.K." Peter stepped back, out of the stall, and John let down the shovel, as slowly and smoothly as possible, then he eased the gears into first, and relieved the pressure of his foot on the clutch. It popped, and the tractor jumped forward, digging the tines of the shovel into the dirt. "Be careful!" called the older boy, but it hadn't been that bad, and John could tell that Peter wasn't really annoyed. He scooped out the muck, lifted the shovel, and backed up. Then he made a left turn, and drove blandly over to the manure pile, where he tipped the shovel and the dirt fell with a satisfying thump right on the spot he'd intended. He turned the rig around. Peter had begun the next stall.

John loved it. There was a wonderful rhythm to it, as if he were a giant, eating very slowly. For a while, four stalls in a row, he had no hesitations, jerks, or mistakes. Peter said, "You want me to take a turn?"

"Not unless you want to."

"I don't."

They worked without talking, because of the noise of the tractor, but John felt almost as if they were conversing, so smooth was their cooperation, so satisfied was he with himself and his job and Peter for trusting him to drive. He fell into pleasant fantasies about driving a car, his own car, anywhere he would choose.

At last they took a break, sitting down in the shade of one of the clean stalls and drinking from the water jar Peter had filled. Peter stretched out his legs. "Seventeen down, thirteen to go."

"What time is it, do you think?"

"Midafternoon, I guess."

"Seems like it's going pretty fast."

"Yeah. I hate to drive that tractor."

"Not me. I don't think this is such a bad job, really. Not like it was when we had to do it with shovels and wheelbarrows."

"Margaret should have learned to drive the tractor."

"She's always been kind of a dope about machines."

"Yeah, well . . ." Peter sighed.

"No, look. If you know how, and practice, then it's fun. I mean, you can only get so much fun out of picking up every little speck of dirt with your pitchfork. No matter what you do, it's got to get boring. And I suppose the tractor would get boring too, but there's just that many more things to learn to do, so it wouldn't get as boring as fast, don't you think? I think that's the thing, you know. To do something that has so many little details about it that you couldn't really master them all, no matter how much time you've got."

"But how do you know that? I mean, before you really get so far into it that you can't get out?"

"You can always get out."

"I don't think that's true."

"Sure it is. If you can't then you're a weakling, but you don't have to be one. You just have to make up your mind. It seems to me that's the best thing about being grown up. You just have to make up your mind, not everybody else's too." John spoke enthusiastically.

"Yeah, that's easy to say, but look at somebody like Mr. Blake. I'll bet he doesn't like teaching science. I'll bet he'd like to go back to school, or make more money or something. Or better still, look at nuns. They can't just make up their minds."

"They can up to a certain point, then that's just it, they're supposed to make up their minds right then and there."

Peter took a drink from the jar. "Do you think having the vocation is the kind of thing with so many details that you'd never really master them all?"

"I think they'd like you to think that."

"That's for sure."

"Have you?" asked John.

"What?"

"Had the vocation?"

"Nah, I guess not."

"Me, neither. Not since first grade, anyway."

"First grade?"

"I thought Father Simon was pretty neat."

"He was, actually. Right out of the seminary they're still pretty good."

John and Peter had never been close. John, in fact, had never felt close to any of the others, and he would not have said that they felt particular kinship with each other. There were somehow too many of them, and they had had to share too many things and too many spaces. Right now, however, it occurred to him how much he liked talking to Peter: so much that he would have spoken about it, except for fraternal reserve and, perhaps, something in Peter that he might have embarrassed. Peter sat with his back against the fence, his knees high, his elbows resting on them, and his hands dangling. John arranged himself in imitation of the older boy, smiling, thinking what a kind person and superior older brother Peter had always been, never like the older brothers of his friends, who insulted, rejected, and beat up on their siblings as a matter of course. To have such a brother as Peter suddenly seemed lucky, and not to have attained a greater measure of intimacy, impossible. He said, "Thanks for letting me drive the tractor."

"You're welcome." Very simple. John thought, with respect, that there was something about Peter that was very simple. "Let's get back to work."

The job should have been easier and more fun after the break, but it was not. For no reason, things had shifted slightly, out of the realm of smooth coordination and into the realm of little mistakes. Even the gears on the tractor, which had clicked precisely all afternoon, now clashed sometimes and had to be double clutched. John glanced at Peter for signs of a similar perception, but there were none. In fact, Peter, like the tractor, had begun to work less efficiently, and to lapse into his customary state of abstraction. John wondered if he would have perceived this subtle change in the tone of a piece of work a week or a day before, and he congratulated himself. It was as if he had suddenly gotten smarter. He felt exuberant, and bounced slightly on the wide spring seat of his favorite vehicle.

Feeding time came and went. They could hear Margaret and Henry slam the doors, turn the spigots, and bang the buckets that gave notice of the end of the day. The boys had done a lot of work—twenty-seven of thirty stalls, and only the small pony stalls left. John still hadn't relinquished the tractor and mother still hadn't appeared. He felt as if he had grown three years in driving expertise since lunchtime. "Hey!" he shouted to Peter. "Let me try taking that bit without emptying this first. It would be faster!" Peter nodded, and stepped back, at the same time turning away from the scoop shovel to look toward the main barn. John's gaze followed his brother's for a second, but mother wasn't coming. When he turned back to what he was doing, it was to see the shovel, which he had already begun to lower, drop quickly, too quickly, and just inches from Peter's averted head. The most frightening thing was that Peter could have been hit (and possibly killed? how heavy was the shovel? how fast was it descending?) without John's seeing, in that second when his eyes so innocently turned away. Of itself, his hand slammed down the lever and the shovel jerked upward. Peter jumped, and bits of dried muck fluttered around him. "Say! What are you doing?"

"Nothing! You're standing too close!" Peter stepped out of the way, and John breathed hard for a second. He was shaking. After an embarrassingly long time (or it would have been had Peter been paying attention) he lowered the shovel very, very slowly, and scooped up the dirt his brother had loosened. The worst thing was that he could never say what he had seen, never diffuse that moment of pure carelessness on his part by speaking of it or making a joke of it. He cleaned out the last stall perfunctorily, and started to jump down. "Be careful!" said Peter. "I don't think the emergency brake's on." Innocent, unharmed. John pulled on the brake as tight as it possibly could go. "What's the matter with you?" said Peter, but John didn't answer. "Dinner!" shouted Henry, appearing around the corner of the main barn. John dusted his hands on his pants and got down off the tractor as if he had every right in the world to be there.

Father, who'd concocted this year's mixture of alfalfa, clover, and timothy, who'd seen to its planting and watched it lovingly for these three months, stayed home for the ten days of haymaking until the high, hot barn was filled with sweet bales. All the lesson horses were put out to pasture, and Louis, who came every year, but whom the children had never spoken to, appeared on his ancient tractor to mow and bale the crop.

Axel made breakfast: pancakes and thick sausages, squeezed orange juice, honey, jam, butter; apples and oatmeal cookies for later. Through the screen came the undulating sound of Louis as he spiraled the back field. Margaret could see him when she came out, stuck far away to the side of a green hill, wiping his face with the pinpoint of a red bandanna, and liable, it seemed to her, to tip over, but he never did. Louis knew every hollow in every field for miles around.

What amazed Margaret was not that he was changeless, although he'd seemed for years unalterably old, but that he changed. One day a different cap, one day a different shirt, each year a different pair of heavy-soled shoes (never work boots). This year he wore white-soled turquoise oxfords, hideous and crazily fashionable. She felt them drop permanently into her memory along with the rest of the summer, as if she were experiencing some final version. "Move it!" said Peter, nudging her teasingly off the back step. Everyone's spirits were high during haying, though the days were if anything longer than usual. Margaret wondered at this too. All her recent wonder made her feel sticky and slow, but she kept up with the others. The horses were cared for at a run, then the children grabbed their bamboo rakes and Axel rode them on the hood of the

Plymouth out to the sun-washed field. Each made a row, counting off parallel falls of grass left by the fork blades, and began to rake.

Breezes eddied about her bare arms and legs. She saw the house, the barns, the trees and meadows beyond. The morning light spilled freshly over everything, and the fragrance around her rose and rose in transparent billows to the vaulted sky. John and Henry tangled rakes. "Out of my way, punk!" John said, laughing.

"Who are you calling a punk? Look at this!" Henry laid his rake in the green stubble, then bent down and picked it up, pretending to be a weight lifter. He grunted and heaved convincingly. "My hero!" said John, and smacked him lightly on the head.

"Heave ho!" called Peter. "Massa'll have the whip on ya!" It was perfect to shout, wave one's arms, move expansively, unfearful of scaring horses.

"Margaret!" called Henry. "I think you're putting on weight." Unwary, she looked down at herself. "Yes, Margaret, I think you can easily do without that oatmeal cookie in your pocket."

"Eat your heart out."

"Oh, Margaret, I'm dying." He fell into the unraked cushion of grass and wildflowers. "Save me. One oatmeal cookie means the difference between death and my destiny. Think of my poor old mother . . ."

"Yeah!" cried John. "Think of her!"

"Think of my leetle seester!"

Margaret tickled him with her foot. "What do you know about leetle seesters?"

They never mussed the neatly made ribs of hay, however, and when Margaret stood and turned, these were like tracks rolling away from her toward Louis, who had rounded the dead tree corner and roared slowly up the hill. He bounced, tiny on his chintz-pillowed seat, and worked without stopping. He passed

53

her. The back of his head receded, then his ear, brown and flat against his head like a slice of mushroom, went up the short side of the field and disappeared behind the rise. He used the driver's wheel not so much to steer as to hold on, and in the midmorning he spread his bandanna over the top of his head. Work, she thought, made use of time so mysteriously. First it was undone, then done, and days were lost, fields denuded, security amassed, and all in present time. Suddenly it was noon; she'd forgotten to eat her apple, and at last had given her cookie to Henry, who shouted, "Lunch!" as soon as he saw father get into the Plymouth.

The afternoon was long and short, timelessly fatiguing. Margaret felt more normal: her feet resented the stubble, her skin the hayseeds, and her ears the noise, but it was still good to stretch and rake and joke with the boys. She found herself grumbling and making excuses to take breaks, and this in a way relieved her. It hadn't been right, she decided, to soar above the work, to enjoy its significance as if it were transient. An owl appeared, and perched on the telephone pole at the bottom of the field. A great horned, John said, and it was enormous. The hoots trumpeted over everything, even the sound of Louis's engine, and it didn't fly away when they ran down the hill and stood gaping. In its giant darkness, with its talons finger-long, it seemed too large and present to be a mere bird—more like a fire engine or a visiting dignitary, Margaret thought. It ruffled its wings at them, but seemed neither frightened nor earnest. It perched for nearly an hour, then flew over them toward the woods, huge and stately in the light and heat of the late afternoon.

Mother fed the horses while the children worked into the best, long-shadowed hours. When father came to bring them in for dinner, the boys sprawled across the hood of the Plymouth and bemoaned their fatigue and their blisters. Father eased around standing broodmares and curious yearlings, and Margaret

54

peered closely at their legs. Pastured horses, especially clumsy and exuberant yearlings, often had wire cuts or showed evidence of lameness. She handed her rake to Peter and jumped down for a closer inspection. The yearlings pressed gawkily around her, nibbling her clothing or skin, scratching the bony sides of their heads on her back as she bent over their legs and feet. They squealed and she straightened up, saying, "Stop that!" though of course they were not dogs or children, and had no notion of what she meant. After she had painted their little cuts from the small bottle of gentian violet she'd brought, they followed her up the hill. Thinking something might be up, the broodmares, foals, and two-year-olds straggled along, and she arrived at the gate with a train of leisurely beasts. She started to cry.

In the morning, they found that Happy Heart had borne a foal, a lovely chestnut filly, with legs like rope and the thick, wavy fur of newborns. The children went out before breakfast to find mother, who was feeling its knees and ankles and watching for signs of defective vision or hearing. There seemed to be none. The mare too was on her feet, apparently healthy, though covered with clotted blood and dried sweat. The filly rolled her eyes at the noise they made and skittered to the far end of the high, dark stall. The mare tossed her head at them, then turned to the foal and scraped her long tongue over its face. Mother stepped up to it, as gently as you please, assuming its trust and therefore receiving it, and guided the sharp little muzzle to the teat. It sucked, but rolled its huge eyes doubtfully at the children. "Perfect," said mother, "and going to be big, I'll bet. We'll call her Happy Holidays."

Margaret got a pitchfork, and moving around the foal smoothly, as if in water, she picked up manure and the remains of the afterbirth, then spread new straw, banking it high in the corners and against the walls. For minutes at a time she stood still in the stall talking, making humans familiar and trusted to what would one day be an enormous animal. Foals were nothing new to her; this was, in fact, the second of the season; but a dangerous feeling of importance about it dumped her back into the unbearable excitement of the day before. "You're number forty-two," she said in a croon. "Nothing about the number forty-two that's significant, is there?" The foal twitched her tail and pressed against Happy Heart.

The day was hot, perfect June again, and the children were talkative in the field, for though the novelty had worn off Louis and the wearing of short pants, they had the pleasure of speculation about the new filly: how big she would be, what she would look like, who, in the end, would get to train and ride her. And there was the pleasure of wagering on the foaling date of the other expectant mare, who'd been bred the day before this one.

The grass dried in the meadows for nearly a week, then father got out the skeletal John Deere and enlisted the help of Louis's son Jack and the four eldest Pony Clubbers in loading bales and filling the barn, which was much harder work than raking, although Margaret still liked it. Louis circled all the fields again, this time dragging the baler, and the two crews of children followed, loading bales onto the wagons pulled by father and Jack (who had brought a greasy Farmall of World War II vintage). The work consisted of concentrated walking and lifting, then total relaxation while they rode steeped in hay fragrance to the barn. Heat and sweat and difficult footing up in the loft followed, then the shock of cool breezes when they came down, always this shock, no matter how hot the day really was.

John bragged to the Pony Club girls that father had picked up the tractor for a hundred dollars, and almost let on that he had driven it one whole afternoon, but prudence stopped him. During the first morning, he half waited for father to offer to let him at least start up the engine, but the topic didn't arise, and on reflection John thought that it might not be smart to be found out knowing more than he ought. Anyway, it was the baler that really interested him. He loved to frighten the Pony Clubbers with tales of dogs and toddlers swept up and later tidily returned: squared off, divided into convenient sections, and trussed with yellow twine. There was Louis with his back turned, his foot on the accelerator, his hearing blocked by the noise of the tractor, and here were the revolving, consuming blades, indiscriminate. The girls shuddered, and so did Margaret, who'd heard these stories every haymaking for as long as she could remember. The success of his narration elated John, who then teased the others further by seeming to linger unawares in the path of the oncoming baler. Once, as he jumped out of the way, he threw his straw hat into the feeder. When it came out the other end in pieces, some of the children blanched, as if expecting to see blood. In this mood, they would scream at Jeepers, who liked to trot along in the shade under the hay wagons, and always seemed in danger from the wheels.

When he was in charge of stacking bales, John could mount castles on his wagon that breasted the uneven ground as if cemented together. Sometimes he would stand tall on the highest bale, with his arms spread, swaying, and Margaret was almost afraid. She was not accustomed to being afraid for John, as she was for Peter (there were early photos of Peter smiling beatifically into space, and her with a look of the most selfless concern for his clothing, his toys, and his peace of mind. Although he was the best of mother and father, and she an assortment of grandfather, Uncle Jerome, and a friend of mother's pregnancy—who bore much the same relationship to Margaret as a hare to a hare-lip—she envied Peter nothing, not the lips like tendrils nor the opalescent complexion. He was so well-intentioned and innocent and tall that his handsomeness seemed like the mark of a hemophiliac condition to her, and she had always feared for his least daring risks). But John? He was short, vociferous, dark, more of a pest than a concern, in spite of his angers and impulses. She never expected him to stumble into anything, even as a joke. He always eventually plopped down among the bales with the rest of them, and she always reprimanded him: "You shouldn't tease the Pony Clubbers like that."

"They love it." He poked her in the side. "You too."

"Not me." But she couldn't help smiling.

"Say, what book did they write . . . ?"

"About eight purple college girls. Yeah, yeah. How come you tell the same prehistoric joke every time we ride into the barn?"

John shrugged. "Hey! Father's paying us sixty dollars this year. Pony Clubbers twenty-five."

"Who told you?"

"Henry."

"You ought to put it toward your new black boots. Mother said . . ."

"Yeah, right. This guy went into a doctor's office and he said, 'Hey, doc, my mother thinks she's a horse.' "

"Your mother thinks you're nuts and the rest of the family agree."

"Who, me?" John definitely did not want to put this abundance, this sixty dollars, toward his new black boots, although he didn't yet know what he wanted. He imagined a street of large shop windows, and the light reflecting off them, so that he could not see in without stepping up close. He would inspect one side of the street, then the other, using a whole morning or a day to do it, and then he would begin again. The thing, perhaps, would be hidden behind something else. He would have paused to look at a tool or a game, and a hand from inside the store would reach into the window display, shift a few items around, and there it would be, the thing he wanted, the thing that nestled so certainly into a whole sixty dollars. He imagined the scene clearly, even once dreamt about it, but as the hand reached in, and the thing appeared, and he bent to look more closely, he woke up, still not knowing what it was.

The ready fashion in which new clothes mixed themselves with the rest of his laundry convinced him that it was not apparel. He did not want a book, since the farm was a wasteland of unexplored books, but, if a book was not it, a book was like it. The colorful cover of a book, the available mystery of a book's pages, the familiarity of a properly chosen book when it was taken up again and again was very like the thing he wanted. He thought of scientific equipment—jars, nets, traps, maybe even a telescope—to explore the farm as he had planned a few weeks before, but these did not glitter in his thoughts as the thing did.

He dismissed records at once, though regretfully, because the "phonograph," as mother called it, was in the living room, stuck into the wall, immobile and public. He dismissed toys at once because he was fifteen and even the word "toy" embarrassed him. There was, however, something in the nature of toys that was also in the nature of the thing; at least, he remembered feeling about certain of them (the model train he'd shared with Peter, for instance, and the wood-burning set) this same assurance that the layers of enjoyment were inexhaustible, and only lack of time and failure of application on his part had doomed the importance of the toy to his life. In their very nature, games implied sharing, and he was anxious that the thing be his alone, to be taken out in private and used secretly, silently. Sixty dollars! It was wonderful and auspicious that nothing he could think of ever having really wanted had cost as much as sixty dollars.

As they rode in on the next load, John pursued this idea. "Look, Margaret, as much as mother may disagree, life doesn't just end at the blacktop."

"Mother never . . ."

"Do you realize all the things there are out there?"

"Of course I do." She smiled. "I mean, look at all the stuff in your room alone. The basketball, the Chinese stuff you had to have. Remember that ant farm . . ."

"Why haven't we learned to ice skate, or ski? That man from New Jersey offered mother eight thousand dollars for Foolish Heart. We could get a sailboat with that and sail on the lake."

"Who told you that?"

"Henry. Imagine that in hot weather! There's this kind of sailboat that's all made of plastic or something and if it tips over you just push it back up and climb on. Or we could go somewhere. We've never been anywhere!"

"Mother would sell Foolish Heart if she thought it was the best thing to do."

"Nowhere! I can't believe it! The Murphys go to Hawaii every other year, and Mr. Murphy doesn't make any more than dad."

"Who said?"

"You know what else? We've lived on this place all our lives and she's never taught us a thing about what's here. We might as well live in the suburbs for all we know about the animals and plants and stuff."

"There's plenty to do already."

"Right! Mother doesn't have the first notion . . ."

"I won't listen."

John was silent for a while, then said, "Well, nobody rides Foolish Heart very much, and she's nearly a six-year-old."

In the hayloft, he stopped her heart and made her laugh by appearing to fall twenty feet to the corn bin below, then whispering, "Margaret! Margaret!" when she hesitated in horror to look over the edge.

SOON they were riding again. The vacation from one another did not seem to do Peter and MacDougal any good, but rather to confirm their disagreements. As the first horse show of the summer approached, Kate grew bitter about the failure of her best rider to get along with her best horse. They tantalized her with moments of elegance, then harassed her by fighting each other. One morning the two of them actually fell down in the middle of a jump course, when MacDougal halted on a turn and reared, then Peter pulled them over backward. Even floundering on the ground, MacDougal could not dislodge his rider, whose long legs hugged him like a leather strap, and whose long fingers still strove to handle the reins as tenderly as if they were spider webs.

For a moment Kate hoped they would kill each other and have

it over with, but when Mac was on his feet, with his ears flat to his head and his eyes rolling, she grew fearful that they really might. The other students stopped talking. Kate, though she wanted to shout some instruction, knew that nothing could be said, and nothing heard. The horse grunted and arched his neck, straining to take the bit in his teeth and run away. He bucked. Peter kicked him and set his right hand, making him cock his jaw upward and to the right. In such a position there could be no more bucking. There could, however, be the folding of knees, and there was. MacDougal lay down again, and with a large equine groan let his head sink to the grass. Peter, white, his left leg caught under the saddle, closed his eyes. He was suddenly so handsome and resigned that Kate knew there was no rescue she could perform. She stood still. In her peripheral vision she saw Teddy cropping grass. The phone rang in the house. Freeway banged buckets, solitary in the barn, and a breeze carried the fragrance of straw and manure past her into the woods. Peter sighed, opened his eyes, jimmied his leg out from under the horse, and stood up. He loosened MacDougal's girth, and the horse lifted his head. In a moment the saddle was off, and the horse being led toward the barn as calmly as could be. Kate wanted to scream. Instead, she called to the others, "O.K. Sit-trot without stirrups! Prepare to trot! Trot, please!"

Peter never spoke about the problem, for he did not share his family's belief in words. He saw daily evidence that his brothers and sister witnessed details and made associations that he never caught, and his suspicion that he was stupid was reconfirmed. Occasionally, during riding lessons, one of the others would have trouble with a horse, and the solution would make itself known in Peter's consciousness, but it never occurred to him to mention it. No doubt the result, he thought, of selfishness, his other besetting sin. He prayed nightly to be released from selfishness, stupidity, clumsiness, and growth, and his prayers had no effect that he could see. MacDougal, though they were getting along badly, was one of the few things in his life that didn't confuse him. On their best days, and even during moments of their worst ones, he felt himself coming to a physical understanding of the horse, so that the horse could not make the smallest evasion or rebellion that surprised him. Equally, he was learning the symptoms of imminent cooperation, and how to control the elation in himself that they produced. MacDougal was perverse and rewarded overconfidence with misbehavior, but he occasionally rewarded humility with unexpected pliancy. Peter, however, hadn't the lexicon to tell Kate about this silent progress, and MacDougal's tantrums masked it completely.

"Peter," said Kate at dinner, after Axel had asked him three times for the milk with no response, "is preoccupied because he's having a terrible time with MacDougal. Henry, pass your father the milk." Axel smiled his thanks at Henry, and tried to fill his glass nonchalantly. His interest in pursuing discussions with Kate on the equestrian progress of his children was nonexistent.

"Peter," Kate went on, seeing that Axel was fidgeting in his seat and desiring to pin him there, "is making no headway that I can see."

Really, she had such a lovely voice. Axel was tempted, as usual, to submit to the truth of everything the voice uttered, to the justice of every claim the voice made. He looked at Peter, but Peter looked at neither of them. He did not appear even to have heard his own name, or to know that he was under discussion. He showed now, as he always had, lithe obliviousness that was a quality of genius or idiocy that Axel had always admired, but it was the same quality that kept him from feeling much kinship between them. "Peter, wake up. Your mother is talking to you."

"It's no use talking to him," said Kate. She picked up her knife with the air of having dropped the subject, as if she had been unwillingly betrayed into bringing it up in the first place.

"Pray for him," said John.

63

"Pardon me?"

"Pray for him." Axel put his napkin to his mouth, hiding his smile at the alteration in John's tone from mockery to sincerity. Kate lifted one eyebrow, but said only, "I pray for you all." A draw.

"*I* think . . ." Axel emphasized himself, knowing that she could not fail to resent his having an opinion at all.

She did not fail, and spoke immediately, as if to preclude it. "If I hadn't seen his temper with my own eyes, I wouldn't have believed it. MacDougal is especially sensitive, and he picks up on it. Every day. No improvement at all. But I don't want to talk about it."

"Which is why you brought it up."

Sarcasm, however, was lost on Kate. She went on. "It's hard to tell who is riding whom."

"Ask him, not me. He's been forming whole sentences now for almost fifteen years."

"I asked him. He doesn't know."

Six words, seven syllables. Definite, clear, musical. Axel wanted to sigh, but at the same time, he knew what "asking him" would have involved. He said, "I can hear it now: what'sa matta witchew, kid?" John snorted, Margaret choked on her cheese sandwich, and Kate blushed. Bingo.

It always surprised him when he defended the children, because they had nothing of the power over him that his wife did. Years of some kind of moral discipline made him contradict her even when he yearned for the pleasure of agreement. And it always surprised him when she showed the effects of him; a blush, a pregnancy, each thing seemed impossible, and none of them convinced him that it could happen again.

Just then Peter put his elbow in the butter. He grazed it, hardly denting the yellow oblong, but his noise of surprise was enough to draw the attention and laughter of everyone but Kate. Even Axel sputtered for a moment. Peter turned crimson, and was overcareful about wiping the butter from his sleeve.

"It's getting bet . . ."

"If you wanted to control that temper, you could," interrupted Kate.

"I want to."

"Daddy," said Margaret, so ready to draw any fire from Peter that it had become a habit with her, "do you want the last of the baked beans?"

And of course it worked. "Margaret," said Kate, turning her head with a snap, "I want you to clean out the front hall closet before you go to bed, and the boys are each to do two bridles in addition to their saddles. Your father and I will do the dishes." Axel smiled. Angular and shining, Kate seemed to him at her foolish best when enumerating chores.

He stood by the sink, running the water hot, certain that the previous conversation was but preliminary to something long planned. Kate seemed to be twirling and bowing on the periphery of his vision, but when he turned in surprise, of course she wasn't. She was merely removing some plates from table to counter. Still, he had looked at her, and she took advantage of it to speak without having to use his name. He longed for the engagement, but when she said, "We need to have a talk," he pretended that her words had been muffled in the roar of the water. He cocked his head inquiringly. She stepped up to him, smelling of sun and hay and horse medications. "Axel" (she said it!) "we need to have a talk about the children." He turned off the water, and she finished too ringingly for the intimacy she desired. Miraculously, she blushed again, and Axel smiled.

At once, in a precipitate change of mood that was characteristic of his feelings about her, he grew ashamed. All their married life he had succumbed to the temptation of badgering her earnest nature (he sometimes marveled to think of her giggles when she still loved him and the teasing of her was a glad joint ceremony). Then he hated the sadism this testified to in his nature. Of late this teasing was so subtle and her notice so firmly directed elsewhere that she didn't see it. It was like juggling in a closet. His shame made him speak without sarcasm. "They seem busy and healthy and fine to me."

"They are. There's nothing wrong with them."

"Then what's there to talk about?"

"Well, what is to become of them?"

Axel scrubbed vigorously, pretending to be thinking of his answer and not to be savoring this, the first moment in ten years that Kate had given voice to an existential fear. He wanted her to amplify, to express, for the first time, doubt (of herself, of reality, of God or the Church; the most sophomoric loss of courage would suffice). She was thinking. She found the lid to the butter dish under Henry's chair and replaced it. Even as she wedged the dish into the full refrigerator, he said nothing, waiting. He felt the blood pounding in his wrists where they were plunged into the steaming water. She spoke.

"Well," she said, "that's silly. What I really mean is what's Margaret going to do?"

He was breathlessly, surprisingly disappointed. In realizing his disappointment, he realized that he must have hoped for some great turning to him that would signal the rebirth of their marriage.

"I'd hate to see her get into this business for lack of anything better to do. She used to be so interested in . . ."

"She's too sensual for the convent. I'm sure she'll go back to college." He spoke brusquely.

"Pardon me?" She grew dignified now, setting the dried dishes in the cabinet with offended care.

"She's too sexy for the convent. She could go to college around here, for that matter, and there's no reason that she can't live at home for a while, if she wants to." He pretended to be talking about Margaret's education, but knew the words Kate had really

66

heard. Her stiffening gladdened him, but then his mood changed again.

Kate said, "I see."

"Katherine," he said, serious, kindly, "she's eighteen. She cries all the time. She needs a boyfriend."

"I would hate to see her get into this business for lack of anything better to do."

"Just think how nice it would be to have four normal American kids. Margaret (we'd call her Peggy) doing her nails, chewing gum, and waiting for her boyfriend to come pick her up. His name would be Eddy, I think. Pete would have spent the afternoon tinkering with the car . . ."

"Nobody's had children like that in ten years. It's much more dangerous than that now. They all have cars. That boy in Peter's class who was killed . . ."

"I think he was a couple of classes ahead of Peter."

"What's the difference? I'm glad ours are safe at home."

"Kate, do you realize how old they're getting to be?"

"Of course I do." She had gotten impatient. "Things are very different now from when we were growing up. Their little friends are allowed far too much leeway, as far as I'm concerned. Anything could happen."

Axel didn't answer. Did there exist a family of children whose agonies were simple? He had been an only son whose ready ambitions had sounded in the usual modes. The Kate he had fallen in love with had been, and still was, obsessed, which was why he had been and still was in love with her. They had occasionally congratulated themselves that, unlike most parents, they had no worries with drugs, liquor, and unwanted pregnancy, but now he feared for his quiet, farmbound children. He sometimes laughed at Kate's anxieties about car accidents (she was impossible to drive with), but he had acquiesced to the measures she took to keep the children off the road; he acquiesced to everything, in fact. What was to become of them?

"Sex, sex, sex," said Kate. "Sex is not the answer to Margaret's difficulty." Axel shook his head, trying to remember what this was a response to. Kate went on. "She has to have some kind of work and you know it as well as I do."

"Yes, you're right."

"People may think they can reduce life to sex, but they can't."

"I know."

"There's much, much more."

"She must be interested in something."

"The Lord Himself only knows what it is."

Down in the basement tackroom, John was singing. "'Twas a dark and stormy night and the sun was shining bright, and the flowers they were drooping in the mud." He went repeatedly to the sink, either to take a swallow of water or to rinse out his sponge. "And the doctor he decided that to save our darling child, he must stop the circulation of his blood. God, I hate this."

"Yeah," said Peter, though really he didn't hate it at all. The dark, ancient leather had a half-liquid feel in his hands that satisfied him, and there was contentment in the fragrance of soap, dried horse sweat, wool, and damp.

"So we dipped his darling head in a pot of boiling lead and we laid our darling Willie down to rest, and the robbers came that night and they came without a light and they stole the mustard plaster off his chest."

"I'm tired of that song."

"Just let me finish. No more on the mat will he tease poor pussycat, no more twang her teeth or pull her tail, no more rub her nose on the red-hot kitchen stove, for our darling little Willie's kicked the pail! You want 'Oh, Tomatoes'?"

"An old favorite."

"Henry can come in on the chorus. I've taught him everything he knows. Blind Boy Karlson, they call him." Henry had tried fruitlessly to avoid cleaning tack on the grounds that he wasn't riding any longer, but to Kate the question was much simpler than it was to him. Tack needed to be cleaned, Henry had two free hands and knew how to do it. "Anyone can forgo privileges," she told him, "but no one can forgo obligations."

"Hey," said John.

"Hey, what?" said Peter.

"Hey, you. What do you think they're talking about?"

"You heard them at dinner."

"I didn't think you did."

"I did."

John began to hum but did not sing, while Peter buckled his first bridle neatly together and took down another. Every movement he made was graceful and exact. He seemed slow but was not, and always completed jobs more quickly than John, who had only the air of compact quickness, or Henry, who never worked hard except for profit.

"Hey," said John.

"What now?"

"You're going to win your division at Barrington, huh?"

"How should I know? You heard her at dinner."

"Well, Mac is the best horse, and you're the best rider. It's only preliminary division, huh?"

"Let's not talk about it, O.K.?"

"He's a lot better-looking than The Train, that's for sure. And he doesn't fart all the time."

"All horses fart."

"When Teddy starts to fart all his joints will burst apart."

"How cute."

"I hope you win."

At this Henry, who had been calculating the number of square inches of leather he still had to go that night, looked up. John was halfway to the sink, watching a pattern of drips his sponge was making on the floor. Henry rather wished John would win. He offered, "Somebody from Chicago will win. They always do."

"All mothers fart," said John, and laughed loudly.

"Terrific," grunted Peter, and there was only the silence of sponges and leather again.

"Hey," said John.

"May I help you?"

"Let me do your saddle before Barrington."

"What?"

"Let me clean your saddle before Barrington."

"Nothing to do, huh?"

"Sure, but let me do yours. Maybe it'll be good luck."

Peter looked at his brother quizzically, then smiled and shrugged. "It's all right with me."

"I'll do it Friday night."

"Fine. Say, thanks."

"Any time." He paused. "Well, not *any* time . . ."

"Yeah, right."

John took down another bridle, and Henry began to buckle up his first one. He had his eye on one of the lesson bridles, with web rubber reins, two hundred and forty fewer square inches, if you counted both the insides and the outsides of the reins.

"Hey," said John.

"What now?"

"Have you spent any of your money?"

"I gave mother eighteen dollars for entry fees. I think she's charging me for those braided reins too."

"We're lucky she doesn't bill us for dinner."

"We're lucky she paid us for haying."

"There are people who get allowances, you know."

"Yeah," said Henry. "Larry Murphy gets five dollars every week, and he told me that his brother gets a clothing allowance. A hundred bucks, the first of every month."

"Shit," said John. "Just let her try to get her sticky . . ."

"How is the Old Locomotive, anyway?" put in Peter.

"O.K." In his hand John held the cheek strap of Teddy's bridle, which was nearly black with use. He began snapping it against the palm of his hand, first the strap end, then the buckle end. Peter was not watching, but Henry saw that, as John became interested in this amusement, he flicked the strip of leather harder, and winced a couple of times. Looking up and seeing his brother watching, John displayed his hand. The palm was bright red, somewhat bruised, and bleeding in two small places. When Henry started, John barked a raucous "ha ha."

"Hey," said the fifteen-year-old.

"Hey," replied Peter.

"What's it like to ride him?"

"What's it like to ask so many questions?"

"It's intelligent."

"Look who's talking," said Henry.

Henry was to go along as well, and actually he did not mind, although he made a show of irritability for Kate's benefit. The Barrington horse show was one he rather liked, because the concessioners were from Chicago and brought to their four days in the country a carnival air. Though Henry didn't speak of the cotton candy, the Sno-Kones, and the foot-long hotdogs, he anticipated them richly, and the anticipation rendered him willing, if somewhat slow, in the completion of his appointed tasks. John, though he was riding in both the show and the combined event, was more cantankerous. Kate was going through a note phase: the usually barren bulletin board on the back door was covered with neatly made work schedules, verdicts on each day's riding performance, and reminders. Thereupon she issued John a bill, which read, "John Robert Karlson, entry fees, $22, payment for new black boots, $28." Against such authoritative impersonality there was no argument, and no

71

defense except silence. This silence John maintained with rooted determination, but nonetheless, the fifty precious dollars became a bundle in his imagination, a bundle that was not his. He thought he saw the complacency of ownership in every look she gave him, and he wanted to kill her.

She wanted him to do very well in the horse show and thought that he might. "You took that fence like a hunchback," she would shout. "Look where you're going!" His face grew red, but he got better. All according to plan. About her own excellence as an instructor Kate was modestly pleased. "Who's in the driver's seat there? Be the boss for once!" A monologue of instructions and admonitions pursued him everywhere, and he began to share Peter's frequency as an object of ridicule on the bulletin board. One day, when Teddy refused the logpile on a second try (a logpile he'd been over countless times), John broke a crop over his rump. Teddy approached the obstacle again and cleared it handsomely, almost with style. Kate smiled. She could see that a serendipitous virtue of her "rigorous" methods was that John had grown sufficiently energetic with his mount. She felt vindicated, victorious. She glanced at him in pride and desire for his approval, but he was embarrassed, she decided, and therefore he turned away.

The huge blue van was moved from behind the barn into the driveway. For each child, one dress shirt was taken to the cleaners and two more were thrown into the laundry. Margaret aired and brushed the black coats and velvet caps; the boys found all the ties they had wadded into their jacket pockets. Black belts were searched out, and thin, cool nylon socks. Margaret was allowed to take the car into town and buy hairnets, talcum powder, safety pins, metal polish, and a new toothbrush (for stirrup pads and buckles, not teeth). The big van was swept out, lightly bedded with straw. Flakes of hay were tied into nets, the gangway was laid, and Herbie, Teddy, and Mac spent an hour practicing entry and exit. Only Herbie, surprisingly enough, balked at the dark interior of the vehicle but there was no telling what MacDougal would try when time was short and tempers edgy.

They piled other show equipment nearby: shiny round buckets, curry combs with all their teeth, clean stable cloths, folding hoof picks, fly sheets with Kate's name emblazoned on each side. They even found three leather lead lines, brass fitted, and the sheepskin nose pad for MacDougal's halter that had been lost three years before.

This was the nature of horse shows: heat and bone-shaking fatigue from lack of sleep and too much to do, dust, nausea from excitement and missed meals, the heightened awareness of a few things (the van, the horses, the saddles, mother). The children focused so hard on these things that they lost any sense of the voluntary. Henry demanded at the last minute that they take his bicycle. He was ignored. Margaret cried. She was ignored, though she hadn't cried in almost two weeks. Peter fell off MacDougal, and he was ignored, though he limped slightly for the rest of the afternoon. John avoided payment for entry fees and black boots. He was not ignored, although he smiled cheerfully and stayed out of the way.

The boots, it turned out, were in Kate's closet. John had been allowed to try them on and to take them to his room. Sometime after that they disappeared, and Margaret could not find them to pack the day before their departure. John was sitting cross-legged under the oak tree, feeling rather good and cleaning Peter's saddle, but when she said she couldn't locate them, he knew. "O.K.," he said.

"Well, I'm ready for them now."

"All right, already." But he made no move.

"Well?"

"Just put in the old ones."

"Don't be ridiculous. They're inches too short, and last year you could hardly walk in them."

"O.K., O.K.!" He tilted the saddle up on its pommel edge, and set the sponge and the soap deliberately beside one another.

"Come on! I've got a lot to do!"

"Yeah, right." The children were not allowed into mother's things without permission, a point which John finessed by remarking in Kate's hearing as he ran up the stairs, "I'll just get them from mother's room, and you can put them in right now."

"Good grief," said Margaret.

"Young man," said Kate, when he returned with the box under his arm. He had looked inside. They were slender, inky, gleaming, desirable.

"In a minute," he said, hurrying for the back door.

"John."

"Yeah." He turned toward her, put the box down. A moment later he stepped away from it. She did not raise her voice or interpose herself between him and the doorway. The effect of her dry brown skin, brilliant gaze, and liquid voice was always to make his wishes coincident with hers, sooner or later. "I'm going to put these in the tack trunk," he said, "then I guess I'll try and find that money."

"You can leave it on the corner of my dresser."

"Sure." Even his temper was stalled until she vanished into the living room for her afternoon rest, and he banged out of the screen door. "Well, hold it up then," said Peter to Henry in the basement, "and get out of the way." The annoyance in his voice, though slight and no doubt justified, catalyzed John's rage. He jerked open the boot box, tearing the lid when it resisted him. White: a delicate sheet of tissue paper partly veiled them. Black: the arch of the molded instep melted into the long shin. Here was the rounded calf, here the flat of the inner ankle. His hand touched the skin of one boot. Though fully lined with more leather, it was soft, damageable. A printed sheet inside said, "These are your new . . ." He took them out and laid them on the gravel and dust of the driveway. Then he stomped on them,

74

ground his heels into them, spat on them, picked them up and beat them against the corner of the back step. Once he said the word "Cunt." His anger would not have subsided if Peter hadn't come to the basement doorway, then to the top of the basement steps. He was mild, distractedly, naturally, astonishingly mild. "What are you doing?" he remarked.

"I'm, uh . . ." John dropped the boots. "I'm, uh, breaking in my new boots."

"Oh."

"She's a cunt."

"Well . . ."

"Don't be so fucking agreeable."

Peter went back down the stairs. In the basement, he said, "Did you put in both bars of soap?" then, "Don't ask me, ask him." But Henry did not appear. It was Margaret who later cleaned the boots, shined over the new scars, and packed them. At dinner, Kate made a point of saying, "Thank you, John, I got it."

Ten dollars left. Nothing.

The sun, at last, had set. The tack trunks were packed, the three horses braided, the pressed riding jackets and shirts and breeches sheathed in plastic. Margaret sat on the front porch deep in her father's old armchair, exhausted, waiting for the right moment to go upstairs to bed. A cool wind picked up, promising at least a shower; Margaret shoved her bare arms behind her and pressed herself more deeply into the chair. Her eyes were closed, and she was listening to the thump and brush of tree limbs on the porch roof. No one sat out here much anymore, because the lilacs and boxelders had been allowed to grow up thick all around, and even in a dry summer the place tended to be dank, dusty, and close. Margaret was alone, and she cherished it like a prize. She listened to the indoor noises of John's bath, Henry's evening snack, mother's last-minute instructions, and the click of Jeepers's toenails across the hall floor. The life they signified was as alluring as the momentary vision of a man pouring wine at a white-clothed table in the passing light of a dining car, but also as distant. Margaret shivered, pushed her hands further underneath the chair cushion, and dropped another notch toward sleep.

The screen door behind her banged, and she incorporated it into her half dream as a little hump in the road, over which she could easily carry this burden of sleep, but then Axel said, "Margaret, shouldn't you go to bed, honey?" and she woke up.

"I'm fine, daddy."

Instead of retreating, he came closer. "Don't you need a sweater? I didn't realize how chilly it's gotten."

"I'm fine, daddy."

He sat down in the rocking chair, the one with the loose rocker, and began to rock. Squeak, squeak. Margaret drew up her knees, sighed, and pretended to be asleep, but he continued to rock, and in fact spoke. "Are you all about ready for the show?"

"Huh?" She pretended to wake up.

"I said I guess you're about ready for the show."

"Just about." She thought to herself that after all it was his front porch, and then she woke up completely in surprise at these new thoughts. She had never ever not welcomed her father, not been glad at his appearance. Guiltily, she scraped her chair backward, so that he could see her, as it was his paternal right to do. "Margaret," he said, "I think you've grown up quite a lot in this last year. You've gotten to be a very reliable young woman. And quite pretty."

"Oh, daddy. I am eighteen," she said, then blushed slightly at the churlish tone in her voice.

"No, it's true. I'm very impressed."

"And very biased. Lots of the girls at school were much more mature than I am."

76

"Sophisticated, perhaps, but . . ."

Somehow, it was intolerable. "Can we not talk about it?"

"Sure." Axel rocked and squeaked. Margaret shivered, then rubbed her hands over her upper arms. In the light from the door she could only see the outline of his forehead, eye socket, cheek, and chin, then the soft collar of his shirt. At such a time two years ago, she knew, he would have begun slapping his pockets for a pack of cigarettes. Camels. Before that he had smoked Pall Malls, and before that Lucky Strikes. "Lucky Strikes." The words struck her oddly. "Bring me a carton of Luckies. Pick up a pack of Luckies when you go." The father who'd said those things seemed suddenly an impossibly historic man and Margaret felt herself established and unchildlike in remembering them. She looked down at her legs, which shone goose-pimply in the light. She had put on shorts before dinner, but had not until this moment felt cold. Her thighs looked strange to her, pale and soft, like the chest of a domestic bird, and she wished she had slacks on. And shoes. She lifted herself and sat on her feet.

"Do you expect to do well tomorrow?" said Axel.

"Oh, no. But it's O.K."

"Margaret."

"Yes, daddy?" How could she tell him that the concern in his voice was unbearable? That she didn't want to be approached as if she were a problem or a sensitive plant, that in fact she didn't want to be approached or praised or considered at all?

"Margaret, you seem to have gotten so passive, somehow. I don't know how to explain it."

"I'm fine, daddy."

"Are you?"

"I do wish you would quit asking me. I'm fine. Really fine. Truly fine."

"You were a very straightforward little girl, as I remember. We always used to laugh about the time when you were three

77

and Peter was two, and he dropped something at dinner, his bread, I think it was. Anyway, he was banging his cup on the highchair, and I was talking, and your mother was doing something at the stove, and all of a sudden you yelled, "Give him another bread, God damn it! He's hungry!"

"I remember that story."

"And then the nuns always used to remark about how outspoken you were in grammar school. A little too outspoken for them, I'm afraid."

"I suppose."

"It's going to rain." He said this with an air of having changed the subject and Margaret blushed. "Yes," was all she could think of, though. She was thoroughly surprised at herself. She hadn't talked to Axel much lately, but only, she thought, because he hadn't been around. In her entire life, there was no one she could talk with more simply than her father, who, at least with her, was the most playful of men, and the most accessible. She glanced quickly at him again, saw again the soft cheek and the loose collar, and again blushed. She was glad that in the dark he couldn't see these blushes, for she knew that he would take them, somehow, as accusations. She looked around the porch. There wasn't much—four chairs with the ones they were sitting in, a leaf rake, a small pile of newspapers, the dead stalk of a geranium stuck in a clay pot. Outside, the handlebars of Henry's bicycle could be seen leaning against the screen. There was nothing in the careless arrangement of these objects that could relieve either Margaret's embarrassment or her perplexity, so she looked again at her knees. She said, "The rain will probably be good. That show can get so dusty." The show was two hundred miles away. "I mean, if it rains there. I guess it probably won't rain there."

"It might." Axel continued to rock. He too was having unusual difficulties in finding things to talk of. He thought that the trouble with having a problem child was that the child thought you always wanted to talk about the problem, so that every mention of the weather became an evasion, and every word of praise became an introduction to a discussion of the child's potential. Axel didn't know what Margaret's potential was. She seemed to him what she always had—a lovely, healthy, laughing girl who looked pretty when she smiled and still hadn't quite grown into her features. He thought she was a late bloomer and was not anxious to force her. It was she, he thought, who met his most conventional greetings with the demand that he not worry about her, so that, in spite of himself, he had begun to. He grunted, almost angrily, and rocked a bit faster. His children were growing up. He was used to their being constructively occupied and accounted for. "One more summer," he said to himself. "Just let me have one more quiet summer, then I'll be glad to worry." He looked at Margaret, who in spite of her years on horseback seemed white and soft, and thought what a strain it was, having a virgin around the house. Ashamed of himself, he said wisely, "Look, dear girl, it'll all be fine."

She started again, and corrected him carefully. "It is fine, daddy."

"My mistake."

She took him seriously. "That's all right." Her dark hair, too long and unstylish, fell forward and she pushed it back. It was odd, he thought, to live with and love so dearly an eighteen-year-old girl that he, at eighteen, would never have dated, or even noticed, a girl like the blind dates he had stayed far away from, whose friends advertised them as being "nice" or having "personality." Living with Margaret, living with both his older children, in fact, impressed upon him how shallow he had been at seventeen or eighteen, when his most frequent thought was that he deserved only the best, and would have only the best, and knew to perfection just what the best was. It moved him suddenly that Margaret and Peter, his own children, had already attained a depth that he, honestly, might never attain. When she said, "Well, I'm going to bed," and got up gracelessly from her chair, and stepped gracelessly past him into the house, he wanted to impart something to her about her nature, about how he had seen her every day since the day she was born, and yet she was still a surprise to him; he wanted to say something about the human mystery of not adding up, something not about what he had learned, but about what there was to learn. He could not. He said, "Good night."

JOHN opened his eyes and looked around the room. He had
been dreaming of water and awakened from the dream energet-
ically but incompletely. It took a second or two to realize that it
was raining, steadily though not tempestuously, and had been
for a while at least. He smiled to himself and stretched beneath
his covers. The room was cool, the beat of the rain rhythmic, and
he felt suddenly freed of obligations, as if snowbound. He
stretched again, expansively, reaching his hands and feet to the
four corners of the cradling, spacious, homey bed. He turned on
his side and rearranged the cool pillow under his cheek. He
brought up his knee, twitched the covers just a half inch to the
left, and, exquisitely comfortable, set himself to fall back into an
excellent slumber. Then he remembered the saddle.

He woke up immediately and tried not to panic, tried instead to go over in minute detail the course of all his actions before dinner.

Margaret had sent him after his boots. He had spoken to mother and lost his temper outside. He had gone back to the saddle briefly, then returned to the house to go to the bathroom. After that he looked for his stock, his stock pin, and the silver polish, which he'd intended to use on Peter's stirrup irons. He'd failed to find the silver polish.

Here he pretended that he couldn't quite remember what he'd done next, because what he'd done next was to go feed the horses, then come in for dinner, then put the money on mother's dresser, then sit down to dinner, then help Henry with the dishes, then it had gotten dark, and he had told mother that he was all ready to go, and she had said, O.K., he'd better take his bath and go to bed, and he had done so, allowing himself to read one article in the *National Geographic* before turning out the light.

Nowhere in this catalog of activities did he find anything having to do with putting the saddle away, yet surely he had not left it out under the oak tree? Nobody ever left a saddle out. It was second nature for all of them to keep leather under cover, especially suède.

Suède! Of all the saddles (and two years ago mother had bought them each a new saddle, each a Stuebben) Peter's was the nicest, and had the most suède. John had chosen a sturdy, not very expensive model with patches of gray, foam-filled, velvet-smooth suède on the knee flaps, and Margaret's had been like his, but Peter's fitting problems were peculiar, and the only one mother had been able to find (in New York) was the top-of-the-line model, padded all over the flaps and seat with what seemed to be an acre of the stuff. She had lectured him the entire summer on not being forgetful about getting it wet. She had complained aloud of the expense, but consoled herself with the knowledge that a saddle like that would last a lifetime or longer. John listened to the rain, shuddered, and crept deeper into his bed. As much as he feared for the saddle, he hated even more the idea of getting up in the cold, going out into the wet, and finding it there, sodden. Muddy, maybe. Perhaps even now it was sitting in a puddle.

And what would he do with it when he found it? Obviously the thing would be ruined. How could he face it alone, in the middle of the night, by himself? Where could he leave it? What sort of note could he put on it, to show that he had been careless, bethought himself, suffered the most severe chagrin? A note would be ridiculous, but even less could he stand the idea of the saddle mute and destroyed, merely sitting on the kitchen floor as if he didn't care. And Peter would know what had happened to it, because Peter knew he was cleaning it for the show. And Peter would be angry. And Peter would be hurt.

He remembered how he had badgered Peter into letting him clean the saddle, and realized that Peter would think he had planned the whole thing.

"Oh, God!" said John, and put his hand over his mouth, afraid of having been heard.

In a moment, he threw back the covers, shivered in the dark, and went to the window. The leafy limbs of the oak tree massed blackly below. Honestly, he could see nothing but blackness and puddles, although it seemed to him that he could discern some glinting thing through the branches, right where the saddle would be. He opened the window and leaned out, but the cold rain in his hair and down the back of his neck distracted his gaze. He could see nothing.

It seemed impossibly mean not to go down and bring it in, and yet he could not. Innocence, he thought, would be by far the best policy, at least until the wreck was found and he was blamed. If only it would stop raining. He stood back from the window without closing it, and tried to detect some intermission of the falling streams, but could not. He groaned and stood motionless. Then, suddenly, there was surcease. The intensity of the shower dropped, it turned to drizzle, then quit entirely. John stood still, his teeth chattering, for a very long moment, then slowly closed his window. In a second he was back in bed, warm, at least, and apparently decided about not going downstairs. The three or so hours before dawn stretched luxuriously, and the rest of his life loomed after them, a block of time that somehow would be dealt with. He snuggled down into his bed. Where, he thought, had he learned so thoroughly to get into trouble? Trouble had come to seem his permanent condition.

They loaded the horses and left before ten. Peter brought his saddle up from the tack room casually, and put it into the trunk. John glanced repeatedly in his direction, but there was no answering accusatory look. In all the conversation and argument about getting ready, the saddle was not mentioned. John felt incredulous and elated by turns. Teddy took his mood, and refused to go into the van until the very last minute. It was a beautiful day.

At the show, though they were hotter and busier than they had been at home, they were also happier. There was, after all, the pleasure of exhibitor status. One was careful of one's number, businesslike with the tack, proprietary with one's mount. Little children had to be shooed away, girls in shorts and halter tops had to be impressed, not only with equestrian skill, but as well by hauteur and a touch of testiness made forgivable by the amount one always had to do. With the other exhibitors, most of whom one hadn't seen since last year, there were rumors to be shared and judgments to be traded about new horses. John made it known that he was only riding Teddy as a favor to his mother, who wanted to sell the horse this summer. "We decided not to bring any young horses," he said to everyone. Beside him, Teddy grunted and closed his eyes. The Campbell girls, who rode matching chestnut ponies still, because fourteen-year-old Lisa had not yet gotten her growth, said, "Oh," and moved on to look at Ellie Jacobs's gray Thoroughbred off the track, a contender for the green conformation hunter championship if ever there was one. "Osselets," said Kate. "That's why he goes unsound off and on. Legs blistered at least twice, I'll bet. If that horse is competing in August, it'll be God's own gift."

MacDougal attracted every knowledgeable horseman and every spectator with an instinct for action. As he clattered down the gangway of the blue van, he made it clear that he had arrived. The set of his ears (rigidly erect) and the distance he put between himself and Peter indicated that this arena was broad enough for any activity he preferred to engage in, and that the choice was solely up to him. "Put him away instantly," said Kate. "Don't let him gaze too long at the crowd." From his stall, he neighed continuously, like a stallion. In his adjoining box, Herbie got nervous, banged his buckets, and worked up a sweat. "Terrific," said Kate. "Weeks of conditioning down the drain."

But she was pleased to have everyone see that MacDougal was back on the circuit, still sound at fifteen, still more richly dappled than horses a third his age. He provided the perfect entrée into her favorite subject, the proper age for a horse to begin equestrian work (five or six, not two or three). "Last forever," she could be heard to say as she strolled off with a friend from Chicago, and John was reminded that this would be the best thing of all. Who could keep her eye on whom in this kind of crowd?

Margaret expected to enjoy this show, for the first time in at least eight years, and maybe for the first time in her whole life. For one thing, she was too old now to ride in junior equitation classes, arguably the most competitive and nasty. For another, mother's hopes and attentions rested elsewhere; Margaret could see that mother anticipated vindication in a number of realms. She could also see that the very crowds, the banners, the highly polished horseflesh owned by strangers, the booths of food and trinkets, the constant gleam and hum of cars, the voice of the ringmaster announcing everything to everyone, the organ music, the horses and riders and babies and dogs everywhere affirmed that nothing at all could be anticipated. She threw a fly sheet over Herbie, snapped one of the precious leather lead lines to his halter, and led him into the sunlight, noting in passing that MacDougal hadn't deigned to touch his hay. She stuck her tongue out at him, then giggled. Lately she had encouraged her new feeling of protectiveness about Herbie, who always did his bit, never made trouble, and was oversensitive to the moods of the other horses. None of the family was to ride until the next morning, and she led Herbie away to find some secluded, and still grassy, spot.

The only other person in the small paddock they had roped off beside the creek was a blond boy of her age whom she had met the year before. He was grazing his horse, a bright bay Thoroughbred, and not the one he had been riding the year before, when she came up behind him. She said, "Oh, hi."

The boy jumped and turned instantly, but the smile on his face disappeared when he recognized her. She stepped back. "Hi," he said, with a tone of finality. In a moment he began to move his horse away, toward the pond. He was a very handsome boy, in perfectly cut canary breeches and a lovely pale blue shirt, who had only been showing for a couple of years. Margaret had never liked him or disliked him. She had noticed merely that he hung around with a hunt club crowd from outside of Chicago, all of whom had beautiful expensive horses and grooms to take care of them. Now, however, she felt odd. Not exactly hurt yet, but surprised, as if she had seen something insulting about herself written on a wall in a place she had never been before. Obviously he was waiting for someone, and had thought she was that person. Still, that didn't explain the decisive way that his smile had faded, as if sometime, when she hadn't been thinking of him, he had been learning to dislike her. Inexorably, and by perceptible degrees, her surprise turned to hurt. He was, after all, very handsome. His horse was down by the pond now, sporting a neat red fly sheet and red traveling bandages. The boy, whose name Margaret remembered was Matthew, looked over his shoulder in her direction, then moved farther away. Margaret had never seen anyone who in looks alone was as perfect. She felt her face turn hot and red, then she pulled Herbie's head up from the lush grass and turned to leave the paddock. Another man was coming in, leading a gray Thoroughbred, still saddled, but with the girth loosened. This man was older, and dressed oddly in out-of-date, wide-pegged breeches and black boots with long brown tops. Margaret stopped impatiently for him to lead his mount through the gateway, so that she could make her escape. He seemed unpardonably slow. In a moment he saw her waiting. "Oh," he said, "excuse me," and flashed her a smile of such dazzling, consuming good fellowship that she in turn apologized and grinned. When she and Herbie got back to the barns, her cheerfulness had returned.

The next morning, when she was dressed up, tacked up, and warmed up for the first class (regular handy hunter over fences) she did not seem to herself to cohere to the activity as she once had. It was a good handy hunter course, with a number of tight turns (one was downright intimidating) and imaginative fences; Herbie was surprisingly full of energy, but her focus was different, panoramic. The Sterling girl was next to the railing with a broken arm, a boy on a gaudy buckskin was warming up to follow her, the ringmaster wore different boots from yesterday's, Henry was sucking an orange in the bleachers. Her path around the jumps was no longer the corkscrew tunnel it had once been. She fully attended to only one fence, a huge post and rails with no groundline and spread with a fluttering tablecloth. Herbie leaped straight over it, wasn't that a nice fresh breeze, those hotdogs smelled terrific, she eased him down to a trot, and was passing the buckskin in the gateway. The rider, probably John's age, was staring fixedly at his booted toe. She and Herbie took fourth. The judge, Mrs. Elliot-Frobisher, said that Herbie was always amazingly handy for such a rangy animal, and Margaret only barely remembered to thank her, entranced as she was by the kaleidoscopic scenes in her peripheral vision.

John did no better in his classes, junior working hunter over fences, junior working hunter under saddle, but also no worse (a third and a fifth). Mrs. Elliot-Frobisher was at least not opposed to Teddy because of style, and Margaret suspected, in fact, that she rather liked him because he was old-fashioned in a heavy-headed, cobby, English way. Except for one practice jump, John did not have to whip him over his fences, and at the end of the day the relationship of boy and horse seemed almost positive. When Teddy farted twice in front of the Campbell girls (Margaret wondered if they weren't hanging around John merely to get a chance to talk to Peter), John only chuckled at him and smoothed the two ribbons that hung from the bars of his stall.

Peter made a stir in the junior jumper class, but not as much of one as the little girl whose mount leaped out of the ring into the practice field, raced across that, scattering riders, horses, and trainers everywhere, then jumped out of that field into the parking lot, leaving the little girl, unhurt, on the roof of a blue Ford. MacDougal took all the fences, as it turned out, but also indulged himself in one of his famous statue halts, every muscle tensed, proud, stubborn. Peter's response was to drop the reins and the stirrups and wait. Momentarily they were on their way again, having been eliminated for breaking gait, but still having cleared every fence with daylight to spare. Upon leaving the ring, Peter got an ovation.

Henry was around whenever he was needed, and as helpful as he could be with one hand always occupied by some sort of nourishment. Late in the afternoon, Herbie placed out of the ribbons in the handy hunter under saddle, because of an unaccountable refusal to take the left lead, but by that time Margaret was so distracted by the general scene that she was hardly aware of being in the class. This was certainly her favorite show ever.

The next day, the Campbell girls won the pairs abreast class and John started hanging around their end of the barn. They were undeniably alike, although not twins. Lisa, the older girl and the one John preferred, had been agitating for a year against continued existence as half of a matched set, but as much as she wanted a full-sized horse, preferably a skewbald or palomino, even she couldn't deny that a winning streak such as she had shared with Beanie should not be lightly relinquished. She compensated by pretending sometimes to be sixteen (ridiculous given her height, which was four feet ten) and offering to kiss preferred boys on the lips. Of this number John hoped to be one. At her own end of the barn, Lisa teased him and Beanie watched.

"Would you kiss your horse like this?" She pecked her pony on the nose.

"We don't kiss horses much at our place."

"How about this?" She walked around and kissed his rump.

"Why kiss horses?"

"Don't you love your horse?" This was Beanie.

"A horse is a horse. We've got fifty of them."

"Peter said forty-two," offered Lisa.

"Well . . ."

"Mrs. Elliot-Frobisher told my father that she thought you had too many horses to do them all justice."

"My mother . . ."

"I kiss Lucky every day." She deposited a row of loud smooches along the pony's side, then patted him firmly on the shoulder. "That's why we win."

"Colonel Stanley says we win because we look like two peas in a pod." Beanie pulled her cap down over her eye and threw back her head like Colonel Stanley. "Two very little peas, my dear!" she bellowed.

"I only kiss girls," said John. Then he blushed.

"I'll bet," said Lisa.

"See for yourself."

"Maybe I will." She kissed the tips of Lucky's ears. "Someday."

"Want a Sno-Kone?"

"Sure, if there's lime."

"There was before."

"Me too."

"I'll bet he doesn't have enough money for three. Besides, you've been hanging around me all day."

"I've got plenty of money," said John. "That's O.K."

"Seventh graders!"

"That's O.K." But then he wanted to choke himself for undoing all the possibilities of privacy, of intimacy on whatever level. Though small and undeveloped, Lisa Campbell was pretty and practiced. There were nooks too in every barn.

"I like everything except orange," said Beanie. "I went to a new school this year."

"Yeah?"

"Look, if you're going to be a leech, you can just as well shut up."

"That's O.K." He wondered if getting a kiss was worth sounding like an idiot.

"Now, don't you eat that," said Lisa to Lucky, smoothing the blue ribbon hanging from the bars of his stall. "Lucky eats anything that doesn't eat him first," she remarked to John, who smiled, as she expected him to. On the way to the Sno-Kone stand he tried to keep close to her, because it seemed as if any passerby might peel her off and leave him alone with Beanie. She gave her attention to anyone: too eagerly, John felt, though in his annoyance he had to admit that when people complimented her on her performance it was only polite to thank them, and if they were friends of her parents, to pause courteously and reply to inquiries. Grownups, he had found, were always wanting to talk about this and that. One man stopped him and asked whether Kate was in the market for a really big half-bred three-year-old, and he had to listen and reply and speculate about mother's whereabouts even though Lisa and Beanie were getting farther and farther ahead.

"What took you?" said Lisa, when he found them at the Sno-Kone booth.

"Jack Dean's got some big colt for my mother."

"We wouldn't buy horses from him. Daddy says you never know where they've been."

"Well, my mother's smart enough to buy a horse from anyone and not get burned."

"That's what they all say."

"Well, she is."

"Are you going to pay the guy?"

Then the five-dollar bill fell out of his pocket, and he had to scurry about between knees to retrieve it before it blew away. Some of the change he got in return was sticky, and then he had to run a little to catch up to Lisa, who was wandering down the aisle of concession booths, inspecting candy bars and popcorn balls.

"Hey," he said, "why didn't you wait up?" but she didn't answer, because the answer was clear to both of them. She shrugged.

"She's nuts," said Beanie. "Guess how old she told one guy she was? Sixteen! I mean, she doesn't even pay full price at the movies if they don't know her."

"Big mouth."

"It doesn't matter. Not to me, anyway." Even as he said this she shrugged again. "Look," she said, "we've got to go get ready

91

for the next class. Thanks for the Sno-Kone." Their next class wasn't for another hour and a half.

"Oh," said John.

"Look," she continued, now polite to him as she had been to the adults, "come around later, after we're through. Maybe . . ." She gestured in Beanie's direction, then smiled, her first real smile all day. His waning interest was renewed. Unlike almost every girl he knew, she neither had braces nor needed them. Hers were movie-star teeth, stained alluringly green by the Sno-Kone he had bought her. "O.K.," he said. "O.K.!" She smiled again.

But Kate had different plans for them. In the first place, they had to be tacked up and outside the dressage ring before 7 A. M. and there were saddles to be soaped again and buckles to be polished. An early dinner was in order, and she wanted them in bed, lights out and quiet, by nine.

"Nine o'clock!" wailed Henry.

"You too. I'll not have you roaming around when everyone else is in bed. You can just get up with the others and be a little helpful."

"I think he's been really helpful the whole time we've been here," said Margaret.

"And why shouldn't he be? Now get dressed, and we'll find someplace nice to eat."

Actually she was quite proud of them. They had shown themselves sporting and well-behaved, and had stayed in sight, or so it seemed whenever she looked around for them. The combined event tomorrow was what they had come for, but they had done respectably in their other classes. MacDougal had even taken a ribbon in the hunter hack class, a laughable entry, really, but good practice in staying calm for both him and Peter. The threat of shenanigans, since they hadn't occurred, made the pair eye-catching, and exposed Peter's equestrian tact to very good effect. A member of the Team, Kate was told, had called him "quite a lovely rider, with excellent hands," and if nothing more came of the whole show, that might, in the end, be enough.

When she took them out to dinner, they were quiet and kept their elbows off the table, although Henry did insist on ordering a twenty-two-ounce steak, and then eating it all. A man at a table near them, not a bad-looking fellow, had looked at Margaret for a long time, although Margaret, it had to be admitted, was a trifle on the dowdy side, with her mannish blouse buttoned all the way to her neck and the sleeves rolled down. Upon noticing the man's inspection, she had blushed quite properly. Further, Margaret had spoken very pleasantly to Mrs. Elliot-Frobisher during their encounter in the vestibule of the restaurant. Mrs. Elliot-Frobisher had complimented Kate on what good riders her children were turning into, and had mentioned her pleasure in seeing MacDougal again. "Always a splendidly unpredictable animal," she said. "Should have gone to the Team, if anyone could have ridden him. Of course, everyone always thought he was a woman's horse . . ." Then she smiled at Peter in approval. Very gratifying, although Peter hadn't the wit to utter a single audible thank you.

They had rain for the combined event, not much but enough to render the ground first slick and then muddy. Peter, unfortunately, was one of the first to go, and though his ride might have been called disgraceful with a normal horse, the fact that there were no halts, bucks, or disappearances from the ring (not even the low picket fence defining its boundaries was disturbed) meant that at least they weren't disqualified. John and Margaret had somewhat better rounds, ending up fifth and fourth respectively when the dressage phase was completed and the sun had appeared, near ten. John was pleased in particular with the arc of his volts, though on the judge's sheet his sitting trot was declared "sluggish" and his regular trot posting "lazy and unengaged." "Wait till we hit the cross-country," he muttered, just audibly enough for Lisa Campbell to hear when she loitered nearby and he pretended to be profoundly involved with the knot of his tie.

"Oh, hi." He hadn't meant to bump her. "Sorry."

"You should be."

"Well, I didn't see you."

"Not about that."

"What then?"

"*I* hung around the barn last night. . . ."

"My mother . . ."

"Your mother!" she said it in a baby voice. "She's not God, you know."

"We had to go out to dinner."

"I'll bet." She made a mocking face, then sauntered off. He did not follow.

At eleven all riders turned out in tennis shoes to walk the cross-country. The first four jumps, which also served as the last four, were set into the side of a large natural amphitheater just below the main ring. Only one had a flat approach, and that was a post and rails hung with knotted ropes sure to fly up in any gust of wind. The other three were more conventional—an oxer and two chicken coops—but each of them demanded a choice between an odd angle of approach and unsure, hilly footing that would no doubt have turned to mud after the first five entries. The first jump in the woods was a rail and ditch, where decoy ducks were floating in two feet of water. After that there were two logpiles, a picket fence with an uphill approach, an in-and-out through a shallow creek (to filter out those horses suspicious of water), a low rail followed by an immediate steep slide followed by a sharp turn and another, higher rail, which meant that riders had to keep their pace up and their eyes open going down the slide.

The end of the woods came suddenly, with a sharp turn into an open field, where the jumps, a Helsinki, a brush, and an Irish Bank, were set in apparently random order. The rider could not slow down, but had to be aware of the red and white flags and the correct course, as it appeared on the map, instantly. The first jump you saw was not the first you took. Then there was another brief stretch of woods, with a gate and another ditch and rail. The last jump out of the woods was a picnic table flanked by two large wagon wheels. "At Blowing Rock," said Kate, "we had to take a kitchen table with chairs upside down on the top. It was four and a half feet high, four feet wide, and nothing but daylight underneath." The children shuddered.

Peter ate his lunch in MacDougal's stall. The horse was acting aloof and excitable, and Peter felt, for the only time that he could remember, endangered. He had ridden more diabolical courses than this one: last year, when he was riding Herbie, there had been a downhill triple no-stride in-and-out of impregnable stone walls. One horse had barreled into the third of the fences after losing his rhythm over the second, somersaulted over it, and broken his shoulder, although the rider had been thrown free and remained unhurt. A course two years ago had specialized in downhill approaches as well. On more than two-thirds of the fences, the ground on the far side could not be seen until horse and rider were in the air. The risk had been more felt than real, but at least five riders had been eliminated, simply because they could not bear the sensation of being launched into unknown space.

Those courses had excited him, though. Galloping and jumping, taking care at high speed, lent him advertence and agility that were usually a struggle to achieve. On a cross-country course, his eyes felt lidless, his neck stretched, his chin as light as a petal floating. On a cross-country course he was practically reckless. The designers of this almost pedestrian course had had to make up in silly jumps for what they lacked in interesting terrain. However, he hated to think of MacDougal over interesting terrain. He hated to think of MacDougal anywhere outside this stall, and himself responsible. As if psychic, the horse looked up from his bit of hay, and caught Peter's eye. Peter sighed.

"Huh?" said Henry, appearing in the doorway.

"Nothing."

"Want another hotdog?"

"No, thanks."

"Nervous?"

"About something. Don't know what, though. It's not a scary course."

"Just throw your heart over and the rest will follow."

"Just throw your head over, and your heels will follow."

"MacDougal unchained!"

"Not a pleasant prospect."

"Well, you were hot to ride him. At Easter you begged . . ."

"Hey, shut up and go get me a dandy brush, will you?"

"Yes, massa."

Now there would be the business of getting ready, a kind of bed of activity for one to fall into. First the sinking into neatness and hurry and self-importance, as well as consultation with mother about time, tactics, and stupid mistakes ("Now, don't cross your own line," she would say, "and this time, don't forget, red flags to the right and white to the left," although he hadn't forgotten that rule in five years), then the waking into the movement itself. Eventually one would be galloping forward, fences would be looming and disappearing, and the possibility of a voluntary surcease would not exist. Long ago an aunt had taken him, along with Margaret and two of the cousins, to an amusement park that advertised the highest roller-coaster in the East. He had promoted the trip as much as anyone else, had agitated with nine-year-old impatience to have done with the Parachute, the Octopus, the Tilt-a-Whirl, and the RoundUp, and get on to the main attraction. He had demanded, over the wishes of the girls, seats in the very front, and they had given in easily to his presumed nonchalance. A tattooed man locked them in, stepped back, released a lever. The clean terror of the ride, the astonishing impossibility of his own presence in that wild car still occasionally made him shiver. He had begun shouting almost instantly and had not paused, "Stop! Stop! Stop! Stop!" He had cried and cried, had nearly leaped out of the car in his yearning for cessation. Afterward, while the other children were taken for refreshments, he was led back to the aunt's station wagon. He had never been ashamed, even in retrospect, of his girlish reaction. It still seemed to him the only possible one. This cross-country ride on MacDougal had the same feeling.

Mother appeared over the door of the stall with the impersonal air of the tattooed man. "Now, you're last in the prelims," she said, "and it might be sort of muddy. What are you doing here? You should be saddled by now. Margaret's already mounted up. Where are your boots? You've had lunch at least, I hope?"

Bam, bam, bam. Even as they did it, it was interesting to note how the questions fixed his intentions and moved him around the stall. Here was the saddle, here the bridle, here the horse. "There's nothing he's afraid of," she continued, "though you could convince him if you let him look too long at the table jump. He'll no doubt prefer a fairly fast pace, but the woman in front of you can be a slow boat in China if she's not right with it. I swear she's so barn blind she thinks that ewe-necked mare is Team material. Anyway, listen, he's going to pull you right out of the saddle if he catches a glimpse of her and starts thinking it's a race, so remember that; and don't cross your line, especially in that crazy field they've got set up between fourteen and seventeen. Be the boss for once, and for the Lord's sake, pay attention!"

"Yes, ma'am," he repeated, "yes, ma'am," whipping around the stall, doing up buckles, handling Mac with vigor and assurance, delighted after all to nod and agree, to be the creature of her voice and her self-confidence. Outside the stall there were other distractions—shouts of good luck, the retying of his tie, the further checking of tack and course, warming up (five rounds of walk, three of trot, three of trot in the other direction, watch out, look where you're going, MacDougal in exuberance bucking and kicking out, beautiful horse, no need for a practice jump). And, of course, the worst was true, MacDougal was not his, manifested no recognition of his hands, his seat, the tact of his lower leg. MacDougal was all eyes and ears. He cleaved entirely to the horses and children and other distractions around him, aware of Peter only as an inconvenience to his exploration of the area and his establishment of dominance over all the other male horses. There was a single rider Peter envied, a tall girl on a brown Anglo-Arab, probably level one, from what he could remember. She was slouching in her saddle Henry-like under the only tree. She was eating an apple and her horse's eyes were practically closed. But then he was in the starting gate and on the course.

There was not the expected lunge forward. MacDougal trotted out of the gate, his ears pricked, his neck arched, his whole posture demanding admiration. "Let's go," said Peter, though hesitant to apply his whip. MacDougal trotted forward, pretending to be skittish, green. "Canter, you dope," murmured Peter. MacDougal broke into a slow canter, really more of a saunter. It brought them to the first jump. The wind had stilled, the ropes hung down. MacDougal popped over the fence, and Peter settled more deeply into his seat. They approached the chicken coop as frivolously, the horse's body cockeyed, his steps mincing, but three strides in front of it he changed his mind. Peter's knowledge of this was pure sensation. Everything about the horse and himself seemed to drop and lengthen, as if falling into a groove. The horse did not so much capitulate to him as gather him up—take hold of his hands, fill the space between his knees, center himself under Peter's own center. His strides before the chicken coop were enormous, voluntary; the jump itself was big but rapid, as if effortless. Almost immediately they were over the oxer, nearing the second coop, this one truncated and crenelated with flowerpots. There was a humming of stop stop stop somewhere in his thoughts, but overlying it was ample and growing curiosity. There were the ducks, the flash of the jump judge's red shirt, and they were on the path through the woods. They galloped and galloped.

It was not that Peter was unmindful of his mother's instructions; in fact, he grew increasingly to feel that he was entirely mindful of everything. Through a break in the trees he saw flickering canary and chestnut, and he knew without reflection that the woman in front of him was making reasonable time, but that he ought to check slightly. He did so. The slide came, horse and rider tilted backward without slowing down, and the slide was gone. Suddenly in the open field, he brought MacDougal back to a canter, reconnoitered the order of the jumps and the position of the flags, then galloped on, making no mistakes. Being mindful, however, was nothing, simply life itself. The roller-coaster fear continued. Certainly he was out of control, although the position of his legs and seat, the feel of the reins in his fingers, were all manifest symptoms of being in control. And Mac was acting more amenable than he ever had before. Left here, right here, slow down, big jump. Nobody was in control, except perhaps the course itself, the time itself. They were over the table jump without realizing it. No one was in control, and it was fine, perfect. Coop, oxer, coop, ropes, this time flapping in a breeze. There were the flags. And now it was over. Peter dismounted, took off the saddle, and MacDougal rolled in the grass. Peter wanted to embrace something enormous: the horse, the land itself, anything unembraceable.

Certainly not Kate, who was approaching with a smile. Suddenly, having done well embarrassed him. He pretended his returning smile was merely a squint into the sun. But her attitude was perfect. "Decent time," she said. "You didn't have any refusals, did you? Now, tell me exactly how you went around the jumps in that field." He did so. "Cross your own line at all?"

"Never."

"Excellent. That should put you first in the cross-country, at any rate, though after this morning it won't make much difference. John was eliminated at the decoy ducks. He fell off. Don't laugh at him. He looks like he got into a street fight. Margaret had one refusal at the last jump. Big gust of wind. I could see it coming before she'd even looked for the jump. Herbie knew what was going on, though your sister didn't. Take that horse in and wash him off good before the stadium jumping. You might do a little rebraiding too. *And don't lose track of the time!* You'll no doubt go first or second, and you should do fine if you've memorized the course like I told you."

"Yes, ma'am. Yes ma'am."

"Well, get going."

"It was terrific."

"Yes, well, I expect so. Go on."

John had a gash across his cheek and a bruise under his eye that was just beginning to swell. "Well?" he said.

"Fine. Clean."

"Great." He was trying to be enthusiastic. "Teddy . . ."

"Mother told me."

"Margaret did O.K."

"Yeah." Peter carried his bucket of warm water over to where MacDougal was tethered to the fence and began squeezing spongefuls over the horse's withers. MacDougal grunted and closed his eyes. "Mmmmm," said Peter. "Huh? what?"

"I said, 'What was it like?' "

"I don't know. Clean. Pretty fast, I guess."

"Yeah, but what was it *like?*"

"I don't know. I can't say. It was fun. Anyway, you did it yourself."

"On Teddy!"

"Well, you don't have to shout."

100

"I just wanted to know what it was like! I mean, you got to ride the horse. You always have and everybody knows he's one of the best horses around, and I just wanted to know what it was like."

"Well, it's like itself. What can I say?"

"Oh, Jesus Christ!"

John fell silent while Peter scraped the excess water out of MacDougal's coat, then untied the horse without looking at his younger brother. "I . . ." he began, then shrugged, and led the horse away.

"You're crazy!" John called after him. Peter shrugged again, then was hidden from view.

Teddy had decided that, as far as arena jumping went, he would not. John hadn't decided firmly enough that he must, so Teddy took the wrong lead for his warming-up circle, knocked the top rail off the first jump, refused the second, took the third, tried to veer off course before the fourth, then refused that one twice. He took the fifth and sixth calmly enough, then knocked the top rail off the eighth, bucked twice before the ninth but took it, then refused the final jump once before sailing over it. "Damn you!" shouted John, still in the ring under Mrs. Elliot-Frobisher's eye. Their time was as abysmal as the other aspects of their performance, and there was not even polite applause as they left the ring. Peter's round had been slow but clean, Margaret had suffered one refusal, but lost no time points. Mother did not speak to John when he appeared in the cooling ring, but he understood that she would later. "It's your fault!" he shouted.

And then it turned out that Peter had won, in spite of the poor dressage round. Of the preliminary-level riders, only he and Margaret had fully understood the open field of jumps in the middle of the cross-country, and only the two of them had not got off course. One badly placed set of flags had been entirely bypassed by every other rider, causing wholesale elimination. Kate couldn't believe it. "How smart of you!" she said, though

101

only once. She also said, "The horse could have performed at level two or three, you know." But she smiled. For Peter, that was embarrassing enough.

Margaret noticed the man again, the man with the all-encompassing smile, as they were preparing to leave the show-grounds. Mother, as usual, could not give up her conversation and information gathering and advising until all her closer friends were themselves departed. While the children loaded the tack and the horses, cleaned the stalls they had used, and found every piece of gear that seemed to have been lost, mother waved away at least a half dozen of the people she had latched onto during the show, making herself, with her fond smiles and "God bless you's!" and hints about the best routes home, the hostess and proprietress of the whole enterprise. She was extremely well known. By the time they were finally leading the horses up the ramp and securing them in their little stalls, it was deep twilight.

Margaret was pitching water out of the washing buckets when he came up behind her, leading the gray Thoroughbred. She straightened, wiping her hands on her jeans, and saw that it was he, and that he was looking at her as he had in the restaurant, as if about to speak. His steps even slowed. He was a very nice-looking man; Margaret suddenly panicked and looked away busily, as if she hadn't noticed him. His steps quickened and he walked on. When they were driving out of the gate, they passed his car. It had Virginia license plates.

In the back seat, John and Henry fell asleep. Peter's dark figure at the wheel of the van could be made out in the rear-view mirror. Kate drove silently, and Margaret stared out the windshield in utter blank comfort, idly conjuring up the man's face, trying, though not too hard, to remember what it reminded her of. Other than the faces of her family, it was the only one she had ever seen that actually interested her. She did not have a wide acquaintanceship, and was too shy to look very much at strangers, so she didn't know why this one face stood out so completely from all the others. It probably was not handsome, but who could say? Suddenly she felt very inexperienced, inexperienced and more. She thought of the expression "born yesterday" and smiled, so perfectly did it seem to suit her. She broke the silence. "I think I'm going to name my next horse Born Yesterday." Kate did not reply, and they tunneled on in the wake of their headlights, sometimes between road cuts, sometimes through trees, sometimes merely into the night. It seemed very late, but when Margaret looked at the dashboard clock, it was only nine-ten.

She made up a story about the man with the smile. She made him wealthy and horsy, but also kind and socially conscious, the sort whose contacts with poor people were not merely charitable. He could work with brain-damaged children, or lobby for the deaf in Congress, or do free legal work for folks who couldn't afford to pay. She put him on the board of trustees for the Fresh Air Fund. She gave him an early, very happy marriage, though sadly with no children, then killed off his wife. Widowers, she thought, were far more interesting than confirmed bachelors.

Kate asked her to drive. After they had turned off the exit ramp and stopped for gas, after the boys had awakened and demanded to know how much further, then, after Cokes, switched around so that she was sitting up front with Peter, and mother and Henry were in the van, when she drove onto the highway again, still pulled along by those headlights, her contemplation escaped her, or rather, the simple pleasure of it did. She could still call up the face of the man, but somehow the cozy quality of her thoughts was gone. She remembered that as a child she had loved to lie on the sofa with her nose in the space of the corner, and imagine that she was looking into a dark little room that only she could see. If once she glanced away, the privacy was lost, and she became merely a kid on the sofa in the living room. Now, as she drove, the headlights lost their tunnel

103

nature and turned again into beams of light, and she said to Peter, "I'll really be glad to get home this time." Tired from driving the van, he nodded sleepily.

"But it was fine, really," Kate was saying. She opened the refrigerator, which Axel had completely cleaned out and washed. "Lovely," she mumbled, but not "thank you." No doubt she gave no thought to the agent of the purging. A childhood with servants. "They all won something or other. They were presentable, especially, I have to admit, Peter. Frankly I never thought." She bit elegantly into a large tomato and juice dripped down her chin with perfect grace. "Aline Elliot-Frobisher was very complimentary. She's lost that fake English accent, though I must say, the custom-made paddock shoes are almost too much, God forgive her." There were two thumps on the ceiling. "Oh, I'm so tired. What time is it, anyway? Would you?" Axel went to the foot of the stairs, shouted for quiet, and returned to find her beginning on a cucumber. "Not a vegetable on the showgrounds. Henry is positively carnivorous, you know."

"Did you take them out to dinner?"

"I put it on the Master Charge. It was the only refuge from hotdogs and candy cotton. Mmmm." He could see that the vegetables were cold, crisp, and refreshing. He almost wanted to join her. The conversation paused while she afforded her carrot a long and admiring inspection. Such a gift for him, this amicable chitchat. She yawned and relaxed and rubbed her eyes with her knuckles, took large gulps from a glass of milk, beneficent milk. It was past one. The big van, parked as yet for less than two hours, had already settled like a house onto the gravel driveway, and in his late-night self-indulgence Axel imagined the children weighing down their beds and everything becoming permanent. He had missed them. He had missed her. He motioned for a bite of her carrot, and she handed it over automatically, without surprise or suspicion. Obviously she was very tired, obviously she was so full of the show that she would have told Jeepers about it, or one of the horses. Even so . . . He handed back the carrot. She took a bite just where he had taken a bite. It was so intimate that he looked away. "Mmmm," she said, the way she once had when he kissed her, "is there any bread?"

"Would you like toast?"

"Oh, no thanks." After all she was as oblivious of kindness from him as ever. He undid the package anyway, and placed it in front of her. Unbidden, he got the butter. "Dry is fine," she said. Every utterance tempted him to transgress their agreed-upon boundaries, every utterance bleached, in retrospect, the last seven or eight years of ardent but distant appreciation that he'd been content with. She put her feet up on the chair across from him. The rounded toes, like the toes of orthopedic shoes, made him sentimental. She pulled the center out of a slice of rye bread, rolled it between her palms, ate it, then folded the crust and ate that. It was a performance he had seen before, but never, as now, with this sense of imminent perfection, as if twenty askew years were about to fall into their proper place and solidify.

"They haven't got good manners, though," she said. "I mean, they don't belch at the table, and they do seem to say thank you more than their little friends, but I'd never noticed before how very standoffish they are. Not forthcoming at all. When Mrs. E.-F. told Peter he was doing well on MacDougal, I thought he was going to fiddle the buttons right off his shirt. It seems like Catholic schools would . . ." Before her was the last of a pint of strawberries. She leaned forward, took a hearty sniff, and smiled. Axel groaned. "Pardon?" she said, but she wasn't paying much attention. Axel realized that he was sweating in anticipation of the next moments. This chance meeting in the kitchen, this sleepy deviation from their routine separateness, perhaps had been enough. He did not ask that these moments result in bed. He thought he would be more humble than that, and hope for friendship. Insensibly, just for something to say, he said, "I paid the Pony Club girls ten dollars apiece per day."

She sat up. "That's ninety dollars." Her tone was annoyed.

His hope immediately died and turned into the wide, precise vision of disappointment. "And cheap at the price. They cleaned all the stalls, fed everything, and gave fly baths to all but the yearlings. They got here at six and sometimes didn't leave till after six in the evening. Charlotte and Ellen rode some of the green horses, and Charlotte taught a beginner's lesson." In paying the girls he knew he had been merely right, not generous, but now, in this moment when the whole history of his marriage seemed available to his insight, he wondered what years of being right had gotten him.

"The experience is good for them, if they want to go for their B ratings."

"They worked hard."

"One must work hard for its own sake and not for the sake of money."

He tried to be sarcastic. "Filthy lucre?"

"Well?" As if the last word had been said, she stood up to throw away the remains of her dinner, to put away the bread, to wipe the crumbs off the table.

"Katherine, you should be ashamed of invoking high-minded principles in order to cheat these girls." As soon as he said it, as soon as she looked at him with the eyes of a sportsman affronted, he knew that the chasm between them was wider than ever.

"No one," she said with apparent calm, "no one is a better sport than I. No one at this stable has ever . . . Why, when I discovered the wrong addition in the point totals at that event in sixty-four, I went straight to the judges without even pausing, without even thinking of pausing, though I knew I would lose because of it. It's unbearable to have to defend . . ."

"Money is different. Money . . ."

"Every Pony Clubber and lesson rider who comes out here gets good value for her money."

"And soaked for as much work without pay as possible."

"Cheated! Soaked!" The words were crimson to her, and he was astonished that he used them. She took a deep breath and drew herself up. "They understand that we . . ."

"We could afford it if . . ." He stopped. How had he stumbled into these subjects that spanned all the years of their marriage? "This place is a monument to waste. I cleaned out the refrigerator today, so I know. Let me tell you about all the rotten food that was in there. Are you afraid of it? Is that why you won't even touch limp lettuce or tomatoes with one or two soft spots, or leftover meat?"

"I won't talk about it."

"People think you have such a death grip on money, but it just ebbs away and ebbs away."

"Why are you attacking me? I'm tired, I've had a busy weekend."

"I don't know."

She didn't ask what he didn't know. She was shocked and fatigued, and he noticed that her hand shook a little as she pitched the strawberry container into the trash. He was still right. There was waste everywhere: wasted horses, growing old in their pastures, wasted clothing, bought on sale, too small and never used, wasted food, wasted tools, books, medical supplies, the wasted talents of his children.

He hadn't thought of that before, but of course it was true. No one had ever asked any of them if they even liked horses. "Oh, Lord," said Axel. There was nothing else to say or think. To go further into that question, into any of the questions raised, was not possible just then, conceivably not possible at all. He tried to think something simple. Wasn't it good to want his wife again? Wasn't it purely good, wholly good to wish for the second coming of their marriage? He hoped so, because lately that had been all he wanted.

ALTHOUGH John hadn't spent many of his summer nights in the woods, shortly after returning from the horse show it happened as he had hoped. He came perfectly awake in the moonlight, thinking of, or having just dreamt of, the stream at the bottom of the mare pasture. In his dream there had been the mares, as well—silent, peaceful, moving in groups over the silver grass. Usually it was hard, even on hot nights, to get himself out of bed. In the sunlight, working, bored, sweaty, he could not imagine how the darkness could fail to lift him up and move him down the stairs, but at the moment of waking, sleep seemed full and the outside empty; no reconsideration of past magic or daytime anticipation could stand against the turning over, the stretching out, the giving in. Tonight, however, no choice had brought him downstairs and outside, but here he was, on the gravel driveway with his shoes in his hand. The odor of hot dust had subsided, replaced by the fragrance of cut grass. Half tipped onto the driveway was the rotary mower Henry had used before dinner to trim the patch around the house. The moonlight was eerily brilliant, making solid geometry of the buildings.

Since the horse show, John had felt wicked and lethargic, entirely rearranged by the words and actions that had flown from him during that event. People had avoided him—Lisa Campbell, his brother Peter, his own mother, who was waiting for an apology and a promise that he would write a repentant note to Mrs. Elliot-Frobisher, "who is my friend, a well-bred woman, and a prominent judge, as you know." At this moment, though, the show and the days since seemed daylit and distant, impossibly gauche. Of course he would write the letter, of course he would approach Peter and make excuses, and accuse himself of poor sportsmanship, although merely losing hadn't seemed at the time to cause his outburst. Of course he loved Peter. Out here he could say that, but (he lifted his arms and spun around) out here what did it matter?

What a night it was!

He got into the car, turned the key in the ignition, let out the brake, and began to roll, crunching, down the driveway. His breathing shook with surprise at what he had done, and once he was going (the speedometer read only five miles per hour, but he was certainly going) he dared not look in the rear-view mirror for fear that he would see all sorts of lights go on in the house, first upstairs, then down. The speedometer crept up to ten, where there was a little red dash. Thinking that this might mean that he should shift, he pushed in the clutch and put the car in second. His breathing eased. At the brink of the hill he stopped, put the car back into first, then gripped the wheel and dropped toward the bridge. He wanted very much to close his eyes, but the bridge swept past, one railing on either side, and he had to press a little on the gas to get to the top of the steeper incline. He entered upon the blacktop, and felt as though he had run five miles. Still, with all modesty, he felt he could say that his first attempts behind the wheel were successful, even talented.

The blacktop! He turned carefully to the right, crossing the center line, but managing to stay out of the ditch, and then he was going again. Mother's amber key bob swung and jounced until he was safely into third gear (he vowed not to try fourth, at least tonight) and cruising down the crown of the macadam.

And so this was it. At Jacob Miller's there was a light on in the pighouse. At the Hortons', a spotlight cast a huge illuminated circle around the central buildings. The Zeithamels' huge grape trellis glowed in the moonlight, and then there was a long stretch of corn and bean fields, a copse of black woodland, and the tiny church they attended on Sundays, with its postage-stamp parking lot and picket fence. He was driving! He was driving! He was a little afraid of the dark drainage ditches on either side of the road, and so he clung to the center line of yellow dashes, but nonetheless he was driving!

The road dipped and rose and swept around curves. The needle on the speedometer neared thirty-five, and though he felt that he ought to at least touch the brake (to make sure that it worked), he could not bear to, and then he was closing in on town. Outside Wellek's grocery, he stopped at a sudden stop sign with more of a squeal and more of a bump of his head on the eyeshade than he wished. The car stalled. He'd forgotten the clutch. He jammed it in, turned the key, and was ready again. With a honk and a rush, another car swept past him as he began to creep into the intersection. He jammed on the brake again. The car stalled again. He took a deep breath, decided against going into town, and turned into Wellek's lot. But getting the car to face the road again was more difficult than he had foreseen. First he had a little trouble with reverse, then he stalled twice. Finally, he got out of the car and went around to the front, to see if he could gain the road without scraping the streetlight stanchion. It was then that he realized he had never turned the headlights on.

At last, miraculously, tires, bumper, headlights, and steering wheel were pointed in the proper direction; he pressed in the gas pedal and moved slowly back into the road, stopped for the stop sign again, very carefully (clutch, then brake, gas, then clutch), and immediately was back in the countryside again, moving into his favorite, third gear.

It was like skating or sailing or flying. Shaken as he was by the unexpected difficulty of certain maneuvers, still he wished never to stop, but to speed past the farm into the nocturnal world of dark houses and moonlight. Everything, it seemed, was out there, and how silly it would be simply to turn in the driveway, and go back to bed. Besides (his palms grew sweaty on the steering wheel) there would be no way of knowing until already home whether mother and father and Margaret and Peter and Henry were ranged in front of the house to meet and shame him. Still, he could not realistically disappear in the Datsun. ("He just disappeared!" crowed a voice inside him. "Vanished, never seen again, couldn't be found!") Besides everything else, there was another town not too far down the road in this direction, with its stop signs and traffic lights, left turns, and other drivers.

Just before his own entrance, he pushed in the clutch and coasted to a halt, swallowed hard a couple of times, made the turn. The right corner of the bumper shaved the gatepost. He stopped again, inched forward, stopped again, suddenly intimidated by the steep slope before him. He pushed in the clutch, began to coast, panicked, slammed on the brake. The Datsun skidded slightly in the gravel, its tail slipping to the left, but did, in the end, come to a halt. John was sweating. He started again, this time avoiding the clutch and tapping a little on the brake. Here was the bridge. He resisted the temptation to close his eyes, and was over it. On the next slope the car rolled to a halt and stalled before he could move. He pushed in the clutch and started again. The engine coughed, died, coughed, took hold, and threatened to stall as soon as he moved up the hill, but by going very slowly and giving it lots of gas, he made it.

At the top of the hill he stopped and got out of the car. Though trembling and having to breathe deeply, he was intensely happy. No matter what was waiting for him at the house, he decided, this moment of terrific happiness was worth it.

Then he was rather surprised to find that such a moment could be followed by others, that he could find himself at the house, the dark and sleeping house, and that such a moment could be so quickly and completely behind him.

Through the bars of the big center stall he could make out the reclining form of Queenie, the expectant broodmare that father had brought in the day they'd returned from the show. Returning to the house from his drive, he had been attracted to the barn by a noise, an odd half-whinny. Queenie was overdue, but mother hadn't been too worried; she was the most experienced broodmare on the farm. MacDougal and Herbie, nearby, were wide awake and rummaging about. Herbie neighed; when John came closer, he could see another form near Queenie's, though it was dark in the dark straw. Obviously the foal had been born, and Queenie was in the process of licking it off. Best, really, to leave her alone with it. Except that Queenie, though her head was up, was making no moves toward the foal.

Inspection would demand light, and the prospect of light repelled him. He was not curious. The pale stars, the moonshine, the exhilaration he still felt in his very tissues made Queenie seem hardly real, certainly not tied to him in any way. A foal was a foal. Some lived, some did not, like everything else. Of course this one was probably fine. He turned away, and stepped again into the night air, which was so gossamer, which was so promising and cooperative. A breeze came up, knocking a torn flap of feedbag against the barn door, bringing a whiff of the

Millers' pigs. Everything was crystalline. You no doubt could go into the living room and turn on the radio and pick up Atlanta, or Austin, Texas, or even Spokane, Washington. Johnnie Murphy, whose father was an engineer, and who got to fiddle with the old man's high-powered radio, said that he had once gotten a Baptist station in Spokane. On a night like tonight any distance was possible in any direction. He hated to go inside and relinquish everything.

In three years he would be off to college. No matter how much his mother hated him, she couldn't deny him that. And in a year he would have his license. No matter what, no matter *what*, he was certain to get something he wanted. Kate was certain, for example, to die, and the farm was certain to pass into other hands, along with the horses, the *Catholic Digests*, all the useless paraphernalia around him. He was certain, after all, to be left alone, destined to do as he wished, fated to be happy. They would all die or disappear, and he would be speechless and content.

There were more sounds from the barn. Without thinking about it, he got up to investigate, and without thinking about it, turned on the light, then turned it off. Queenie had stood up. While his eyes were readjusting to the dark, the foal squeaked. It was stupid to look, stupid even to wonder about the animal interchange that was going on. His certainty, his happiness, was rarer than this, and deserved to be cherished. Besides, the foal was alive, making noise, fine. He went outside again, this time distancing himself from the barn, MacDougal's bangings, and any more squeaks.

Except that he was immobilized. His sense of the sky, the stars, the auspicious future had vanished. Although he cared less for any equine in the world than he did for the old tractor or the Datsun, although he didn't find in them even the economic interest that Henry did, he was struck. It was as impossible to go into the house as it was to go back to the barn and turn on the light. "Fuck!" he whispered, kicking the tree he was standing near. "Fuck, fuck, fuck." Nothing, now, could be saved. Kate was everywhere, even where her names were not stamped, taped, or sewn in. In the posture of every horse, the joining of every board, the grassy space around every tree, was the necessity for invoking her aid. In what he knew about mares and foals as well as what he did not know was the certainty that, if he woke her up, she would know how to fix the situation. Furthermore, the ingrained habit of doing so was as old as he was. A foal was a foal, and when he went back into the barn and looked at it through the bars, he said, "Don't die. Just don't die." Queenie had moved far away from it, to the back corner of the stall. The moon had declined sufficiently so that it was now shining through the stall window, but what could he tell by moonlight? Then it seemed better to know than not know, so he laboriously pulled the barn door to, and switched on the light.

The baby's back legs, still attached at the chestnuts, were stretched out and sadly deformed. The hooves were clubbed, bent awkwardly backward. The forelegs were still caught in the amniotic membrane, though the mare had apparently licked the head and neck free. The ribs, countable, expanded while he looked, and the foal gave another of its pitiful squeaks. It seemed very large, possibly because it was stretched out, or because it was past term. Near its head lay the afterbirth and a pile of manure. It was then that he noticed how dirty the stall was, as if it hadn't been cleaned in days. All the straw was mucky and wet, trodden flat, black. Whose fault? His? Though he couldn't remember, the answer would be jotted in black and white on the chore bulletin board in the kitchen.

The foal squeaked again, Herbie neighed, and he switched off the light before opening the door, drenching himself in sudden darkness. He was very afraid. The ghastly and malevolent foal grew very large, seemed to cover the floor of the stall, to encroach on the cringing mare, to tap with its horrible hind hoof on MacDougal's stall, with its enmeshed front knees on the partition between itself and Herbie. Everything stank of blood and manure. The ribs had expanded, were still expanding. And contracting. Its breath got enormous, subsumed the breath of the other horses, his own breath, made them all breathe in unison. He swallowed, then swallowed again. At last he opened the barn door, as quietly as previously he had closed it, and stood solitary in the moonlit driveway.

Now was the time to run into the house and shout for Kate, but as with Peter's saddle, he could not. The thought of having his nighttime presence abroad discovered and questioned was unbearable, and unbearable too was the idea of breaking the silence all around him. The foal, he knew, would not be saved. Its back feet were too deformed for salvation to be worth it, either to mother or to the animal itself, but something dictated that he make the fuss, rouse the family, do what seemed to be the right thing. Even so, he could not. Nothing was saved. With perfect stealth, but having to swallow continually and make himself breathe, he crept back into the house, up the stairs, into his bed. Jeepers thumped his tail. The dog had made himself a nest at the foot, where he wasn't allowed, but John paid no attention. He breathed and breathed, and fell asleep dreaming that the foal had followed him up the stairs. He woke up thinking he saw something in the doorway, then lay on his back, his eyes wide open, until morning.

He heard the others get up one by one. First father, who went downstairs to put on the coffee, then Margaret, then mother, who slammed the back door as she went out. In the bathroom, Margaret washed her face and brushed her teeth, stumbled over something in her exercise sandals, caught her balance. "O.K.!" she shouted. "Now's the time! Don't forget that today is corn, not sweetfeed. Peter, bring in the geldings!" The back door slammed again, at last. Footsteps to the bottom of the stairs, then a muffled "Margaret!" John groaned and put his feet to the floor.

Margaret's distraction had persisted since the horse show. She felt a kind of humming serenity. She hadn't wept in days, weeks; Margaret the Weeper was an alien being of whom she rather disapproved. These days the smallest details attached her to themselves. If there was sadness or dissatisfaction within her, anything diverted her from it. How had it not always been this way?

Sometimes, maybe once a day, she thought about the smiling man, and made up a little fantasy about seeing him later in the season. Such a fantasy was more alluring for the fact that he had probably gone straight back to Virginia days ago, and so she was free to populate all the coming horse shows of the summer with him and not fear embarrassment. She had been like this twice before, once in high school about a boy a grade ahead of her, and once in college about a member of her geology class. Such self-propelled love affairs were entertaining and faded graciously, leaving behind a fondness for these men that made her feel selfless and full of virtue. She wished only that she had somehow learned the man's name.

And she noticed that she had become a good daughter. Her eyes opened before the alarm and ranged over the walls of her neat room. The pictures on the walls were straight; rose drapes that had spent her infancy in the living room hung crisp to dustless sills. Every drawer, every door was thoroughly closed, every item of clothing hung up or tucked into her laundry bag. The floor, after all these years, was free of boots, shoes, fogged tumblers, face-down books split at the back. By the window was a plant, only a coleus dug from the garden, but it was actually growing. Beneath her, beneath the mattress and the box spring, under the dust ruffle, there was exactly nothing. Nothing under the bed for the first time in as long as she could remember. When, at exactly the proper moment, she set her feet in a patch of sunlight on the floor, she not only did not have to kick anything aside, she could see her shoes, instep to instep beside the dresser, and her blouse, still eminently wearable on the second day, hung smoothly over the back of the desk chair. As she stood up, she reminded herself of a very spruce lily rising, at last, from the muck of her own childhood, which seemed to have ended sometime during the horse show.

Perfection was just within reach: certain to follow the washing of her face and the brushing of her teeth, the donning of clean underwear and clothes worn to just the proper degree the day before. It was true that she stumbled in the bathroom when she wanted to be perfectly silent, but it was a tiny mistake that blocked little of the perfect morning she hoped to achieve. In the kitchen today there was even the perfect breakfast: a quarter of a canteloupe, whole-wheat bread, cream cheese, and milk purchased at the dairy just yesterday. "O.K.!" she called. "Now's the time!" When she was sure she could hear them all, she went back to her room to get dressed and make her bed.

"Margaret!" said mother from the bottom of the stairs. Her tone was odd, neither commanding nor monitory, almost, in a way, conspiratorial. Margaret grew afraid and hesitated in her dressing. "Margaret!" This time it was louder, more usual, more exasperated. "Yes! Coming!" she called, zipping her pants and grabbing her oxfords.

The foal lay bloody and inert in the muck, half netted in the amniotic sack, its visible eye open and opaque. In the corner of the stall near the window lay the mare, also still, also bloody. Kate opened the door, but the mare did not stir, and Margaret lifted her eyebrows. "Both," said Kate, "though Queenie's still warm. But look." She raised the animal's crusted tail. The vaginal opening was stretched, terribly torn, black with dried blood. "Too big," said Kate. "Three weeks past term, and there's why." She pointed at the foal's grotesque back legs.

"I don't under . . ." said Margaret, and for the first time Kate showed anger.

"Listen," she snapped, "sometimes when it's not right, they abort it, sometimes they carry it longer, as if it could somehow be made right."

"Oh."

"I should have known."

"Well, you . . ."

"Be quiet. Who's in charge of the stables this month?"

"I am."

"Who's supposed to be cleaning this stall?"

"I don't know. It's on the list. I'll look right now, if you want."

"Too late."

"Oh."

"It's a disgrace."

"I know, I . . ."

"Don't apologize. Just think very hard about it, all right?"

"Yes, I . . ."

"You'd better get this cleaned up. And move those two. They're anxious enough as it is."

"I will, I . . ."

"Well, do it, then."

As usual, it was impossible to express sympathy to mother; Queenie had been one of Kate's first and most preferred broodmares, proof of her contention that considerable talent lay outside the realm of the Jockey Club. Margaret found a halter and lead rope and led Mac to the fence of the warm-up ring, where she tied him. When she went back for Herbie, Mac reared and broke his lead, and when she returned he was trotting gaily around the ring, snatching leaves off the apple tree in the middle, and bites of grass from underneath the fence. She got to the open training field gate before he did, but he was stubborn about coming, even though no one had been fed and she offered

him corn. Finally she bellowed, *"Peter! Peter!"* Always so slow!
"Peter!"

"Well, what!" He was shouting from the kitchen window.

"Will you come out here please and help me with your horse?"

"What's he doing out of his stall anyway?"

"I'll *show you!*" At the sight of the mare and the foal (which was
already shrunken, somehow, already bony, even leathery, after
just six or eight hours since a birth the thought of which made
them both shudder) Peter grew silent and helpful.

Soon everyone was outside, and it was known that John and
Henry had both been assigned to the mare's comfort. The task
had fallen between them as between two stools. Recriminations
began in the house, but were thoroughly squelched, first by
Kate, who said they were irrelevant, then by Axel, who said they
were childish. The sight of so much blood and dirt and pain
made everyone slow and dumb, so that they were only beginning
chores when the first car arrived. Father said they would have to
bury the animals, and he had just gotten the tractor out.
Margaret hated to think of the lesson girls and their mothers
oohing and ahing over the accident, their respect for mother
perhaps diminishing, as though foals, and even mares, weren't
lost on the most-expensive, best-equipped horse farms. But it
was no use. Every time she came out of the barn, another car was
pulling in. "What's the matter? What's the matter?" and the story
was told over and over and over, and everybody had to have a
look.

The morning lesson began long past nine, and John did not
participate. He and Henry were to help father with the burial of
the mare and foal. John did not dare ask why mother didn't
simply call a livestock disposal company. He and Henry weren't
speaking to one another. When father carried the foal out in his
arms, they stood elaborately aside, and when they had to help
one another attach lines to the mare's forelegs, their courtesy

completely interfered with the knots. Father yelled at them to get out of the way and did the ropes himself. Somehow this was the most shocking thing, for father never yelled.

John stood tightly against the stall door, trying to think nothing. Father tested the knots with a few jerks, straightened the canvas he had spread in front of the door (the boys were to hold the corners of it down as the mare was pulled out of the stall, then fold them up and tie them over the corpse), and climbed onto the tractor. John tried to think that after all it was just a horse, one of too many, one of mother's hydra heads. The tractor sputtered, died, started up, and John could hear it on the gravel before he could see it move. The ropes tightened. Henry knelt down beside his corner, abashed by father's temper into preparing himself. The ropes tightened further, creaking slightly, but there was no movement, only tension. Queenie, John tried to think, was kind of old anyway, almost eighteen, really too old to have been bred, and then the mare's forelegs stretched out, and the neck; the nose twisted and came to touch the knees. There was a sucking sound, smooth slipping in the muck, and the mare started. But then something got caught in the doorway—a hoof it was—and father was pressing the accelerator and not looking, and the pastern joint and knee were bending and the head seemed to be straining toward the canvas, rising off the ground. The boys squirmed, then Henry shouted and John ran forward to tell father to stop. After they straightened the hoof and leg, and held the canvas down where it wanted to curl up, John started to cry, though he told himself that this was only a stupid horse. There was no way not to think of the mare in the moonlit dark, standing steadily, her eyes on him.

Soon Henry was crying, probably because John was, and the mare was on the canvas. Father paused, and then lifted the corners, tying them together with baling twine through the grommets. The pink roundness of the mare's muzzle showed where the flaps gapped open in the front, and the bloody white tail dragged in the driveway, its sinews already too rigid for them to fold it discreetly on top of the bundle. They sniffled and followed the slow-moving package, stooping to remove sticks and large stones from its path, and to lift the head over the edge of the concrete wash rack, closing the upper halves of a few stall doors upon suspicious equines within.

The canvas must have ripped, because bits of hide, then red morsels of flesh smeared a trail on the rough concrete. The horse was heavy, the surface uneven, the canvas thin. John grew afraid, as he had in the night, imagining the mare's lower side a gaping cavity, red, organ filled, slippery, perhaps still warm very deep within, as if death were a seepage from the outside, and the heart had only just stopped beating, and the brain still knew him. Father stopped again, and John ran forward to open the double gates into the back pasture.

Something caught, apparently on the two metal gate stops, canvas, or something worse. The bundle would not budge. Father set the emergency brake, and then they had to find more rope, and slip it in loops under the horse. Henry tied one end to a rafter of the gelding shed, father checked the knot, then he and the two boys ("It's too late to cry," he said, "so cut it out") threaded the other end through the top slats of the corn bin. John was allowed to get up on the tractor and put it in gear. ("Don't jerk it, and remember where the brake is. If it dies, that's O.K. this time.") It didn't die, though John was careful to pretend that he knew nothing. Father and Henry pulled hard on the rope, the hindquarters lifted a little, then a little more. Father shouted a breathless "O.K.!" and John released the clutch. When the tractor had just barely moved, father shouted "O.K.!" again, and he jammed the clutch back in. Axel and Henry were leaning against the grain bin, wiping their red faces on their shirts. In a moment, father moved the mare into the field. She slid more easily on the grass. The gate stops glistened wet; John tied the gate shut, then ran to catch up.

There was a cleft at the bottom of the pasture, where a shed had once stood; the footing was bad, the grass sour, and the geldings who roamed the pastures were unlikely to venture nearby. Father untied the mare and went back for the two-wheeled wagon with the shovels and the foal. It was hot. Flies disappeared into the gap at the front of the canvas and found the moisture of the mare's eyes, the mucus left in the nostrils. Others settled on the gory tail. The boys moved away, though it was uphill and into the sunshine. There was nothing to say. Their faces were strained and stiff, but they had stopped crying.

"You said when we got home from the horse show that you would do all the stalls in that barn for a week," remarked Henry, more out of obligation to the absence of authority than real self-justification.

"I did not."

"You told Margaret that."

"And she said we could both do the mare's stall and that's what she wrote down on the assignment sheet."

"You said you would."

It was boring to go on, and Henry didn't feel any antagonism anyway. He almost never did, especially toward John, whom he rather liked because of his unremitting interference with mother's self-satisfaction. "Do you think mother'll get any insurance money?"

"How should I know?"

But then it was too hot even to go on with that.

John sniffed profoundly, and wiped his eyes. He wiped his eyes again. "It's just a horse," remarked Henry. "You don't even like horses that much."

"A lot you know."

"More than you think." This was just a bluff. Henry thought that really he didn't know much, but it wasn't right to admit it. Finally he observed, "There was a light on in the barn last night."

"Huh?"

"There was a light on in the barn last night. First it went on and then it went off."

"Bullshit."

"I saw it."

"Your room isn't even on that side of the house."

"I was in the bathroom."

"Bullshit." John was peering carefully at the grass between his feet, as if seeking four-leaf clovers, except that there wasn't any clover anywhere nearby.

"I did," returned Henry, with more nonchalance than he felt, since he had been half asleep, and it might not have been last night at all. Though it seemed like last night when he thought about it, John was like mother—very definite and persuasive just in the modulations of his voice.

"Shit, what's the matter with you?"

"Nothing, I . . ."

"You're always poking around looking for things and seeing things. Why are you so nosy all the time? You think you know everything and you don't know bullshit." He seemed actually angry.

"I saw . . ."

"You saw. Well, take a look at this!" The fist was imperfect, because John was unused to fighting. He hadn't hit anyone in ten years, since the early rivalries with Peter. He smacked Henry on the cheek, hard enough to leave marks of his knuckles across the bone. The younger boy, surprised, shouted, "Hey!" and dove at John's stomach. They were pushing each other and rolling around when, with the roar of the tractor, father reappeared.

He made them dig. The ovals on Henry's cheek, three of them, turned red, then purple, and swelled slightly. Father didn't say anything, however, except "If you've got that much energy, then you'll get this thing dug before lunch." He had brought water, too. They could see it in the back of the wagon, near the foal, but they didn't ask for any, and he didn't offer.

AFTER the Fourth of July, the farm grew more serious: blossoms were now small hard fruit on the apple and pear trees, the dandelions had feathered and blown away, camomile and clover were dusty and without fragrance. Everything around the children was the hard green and white of middle summer. As usual, they stood on the roof of the barn to watch the fireworks of neighboring towns, although this year Kate made them get down inside of fifteen minutes because since the death of the foal she didn't think they ought to be enjoying themselves that much. She had canceled all their entries in the second show of the season, this one a hundred miles north (often, in the past, a cool and refreshing vacation from daily intensifying summer heat). She spoke of responsibilities and privileges and they put their bathing suits back in their dressers. They resigned themselves to waiting for show number three.

Henry pedaled successfully up the far side of the hill, and then even had the energy to wheel down the road and out the gate. Out the gate, onto the blacktop, and the blacktop unfurled beneath him like a revelation. It was smooth! He laughed that he had never thought of it before. All his life he had heard, "Stay off the blacktop, don't trot on the pavement." The whole network of slender bones and threadlike tendons and delicate muscle that went to make up the four legs of a horse was put in jeopardy by blacktop. There was nothing that blacktop couldn't do to a joint. But then, here he was on wheels, hardly pedaling at all, careless of ruts because there weren't any, letting the sway of his torso make a slalom of the road, going, despite the balloon tires, fast!

When he came to the small concrete bridge that crossed the creek, indicating the northern boundary of the property, he stopped and put his feet down. A car was approaching. He wrestled his bicycle off the bridge into the weeds. The car beeped at him, anyway. He waved. When the car had gone, he was still afraid of the bridge, but also reluctant to turn back. Across the bridge, of course, down the road around numerous but inconsequential curves (distance was meaningless once you were off mother's property) was town. Between all towns were more blacktop roads. Speed, then, would be possible everywhere, anywhere.

He laid down the bicycle, sat in the weeds, listened to the creek splash over the rocks and concrete blocks beneath the bridge, chewed sour grass, but did not cross. Two cars converged from opposite directions. They slowed. One stopped, the other crossed, then the first one crossed. How then did they know which would stop and which go first? It was a question he had never considered when driving with mother or father, but now such knowledge seemed to symbolize everything that could be learned on the other side of the bridge. He would need money and food, and he had none of either with him. He turned back from the bridge, thinking of ways to get both, and down the steeper hill he held his feet free of the pedals for the first time ever. He blazed between the concrete abutments at the bottom of the drop, eyes watering, ears ringing. At some point there was a wobble, but it failed to deflect him. Everything was perfect.

Kate considered herself aggrieved and angry about the muck the foal had died in. After all these years of training and care with the children, she thought she was disappointed in them for letting her down as paid help would not have. She thought she was expressing this disappointment by hardly speaking to them except to criticize or instruct, but actually her real attention was elsewhere. It was, in fact, with Axel, who was subtly and unaccountably flirting with her.

All of that had been wound up and set aside ten years before. The end had come, not without sorrow for her, after a long struggle over his soul. She had loved that soul, and the good nature, the graceful carriage, the shock of blond hair that went with it. No one had ever made her laugh the way Axel had, teasing her, tickling her, playing jokes upon her and upon himself, contriving with her a hidden, very private life, as if they were clandestine lovers rather than the legal parents of one, two, three, then four children. Births of children and deaths of parents, the financial obligations of the farm, frightful accidents that happened regularly to friends, the horses of friends, the children of friends, even to themselves, all of these had meant sadness but never solemnity, the froth of worry but never compelling anxiety. Her conversion had somehow brought the intrusion of high seriousness into their marriage.

When the soul had become one of their concerns, it had turned out to be not simply a matter of Kate's taking the children off to Mass every Sunday, and enrolling them in

Catholic schools (which possibly were better, anyway). It had turned out that Kate developed a passionate intolerance for the prospect of Axel's exclusion from heavenly bliss. "You *will* go to Hell," she said, "you *will*. It's a simple fact." And he laughed. The lightness, the thoughtlessness of that laugh echoed the laughter that had spilled out of her continually from the first day of their courtship. It was shallow, ignorant. It made her think of the other intimacies they had shared—not her marital duties, exactly, but the stealth and ardor of them, and she recoiled. That phase of her life came to seem aberrant, some-how, as if it would have been all right only if they'd gotten bored together. He continued to tease her. Once he said, "You are truly the most puritanical Catholic I've ever seen. The Church *forgives*, remember?" But she thought he was condescending, and shrank away. Resolute, as always, she relinquished the battle, the husband, the possibility of a normal marriage, and now he was flirting with her.

He came in for dinner early, while she was still stirring the Velveeta Welsh Rabbit, and said, "I walked down the street and turned into a drugstore." He went on to the bathroom. "Pardon me?" said Kate, but he didn't repeat himself.

At dinner he was talking to Peter, and he referred to "your dear mother." Peter started and looked at her. The other children fidgeted in their chairs, but he didn't sound sarcastic. He complimented her on the food, although everyone, herself included, knew it was awful. On the other hand, he did not offer to do the dishes, and he absented himself after dinner, when it was apparent that she would be alone in the living room.

Other events distracted her. The vet had to come for some kind of eye infection among the yearlings. Henry stepped on a bee, and his lips and eyelids swelled alarmingly, so he had to be rushed to the doctor for shots, then kept in bed for the afternoon. It was hot and he demanded constant drinks of water. He developed a fever. It went down. She made instant pudding, butterscotch, but he complained of the skin on its surface. She asked him why he had taken his shoes off in the first place. He said that he wasn't hungry. She asked him why he was so infuriating, and he asked her why she was. When Axel came home that night, she was already in bed. She caught herself listening through the wall to his nighttime preparations.

Then she forgot about it, until she began finding things. They were not affectionate things or sentimental things. First it was one of his shoes on the floor of her bedroom, then a copy of *The Economist* on top of her stack of horse magazines in the living room. Two days after Henry's recovery, she went into the hall closet to get her rain slicker and found his muffler in the pocket. These were hardly offers, much less gifts. Instead they were incursions into her territory, expressions of some inclination that was not yet clear. That evening he called to say he would be late getting home from work. "Well?" she asked Margaret.

"Nothing. That's all he said."

"But he's always late from work."

"Yup."

At last there were a number of gifts. She had put a list of "Absolute Necessities" on the bulletin board: socks, two brassières, rust-colored thread, saddle soap, measuring spoons, thumbtacks. The list disappeared during the day when the vet came back to check on the yearlings, and then, that evening, she found on the floor of her closet six pairs of socks (white, Bonnie Doon), two Bali bras (with lace), two spools of thread, glycerin saddle soap, five measuring spoons of stainless steel, and two packs of thumbtacks. Nothing, she could see, had been bought on sale, but what could she say? The bras drew her gaze, then the tentative touch of her fingertips. All of hers were white cotton. All of Margaret's were white cotton. She had seen nothing like these since sorting out her mother's lingerie years before. She dropped them in her underwear drawer and stirred them around with her hand. They did not mix.

The next day there were a dozen eggs in the refrigerator and a new bag of carrots in the vegetable keeper. The beginnings of the week's grocery list, which still had five days to build, said, "eggs, carrots." He neither looked at her more than usual nor smiled nor spoke, but he was waiting for some communication. At first she could not bring herself to make it. Then she found another shoe in her bedroom, this one under the bed. On the grocery list, she wrote, "pâté de foie gras with truffles." Not long thereafter a small triangular can, haughtily wine colored, appeared on the kitchen table. She smiled in spite of her annoyance.

She really did not have time for this. In the first place, he knew there was another horse show in a week and a half, and then, not two weeks after that, they had to be ready for their own show, a two-day affair with an elaborate combined event planned for a third day. The well-known judge Talbot Light was coming. Many of the Pony Clubbers were riding every day now, so the morning lesson often ran three hours (Axel might realize, if he thought a moment, that it was truly a pain in the neck trying to get these children on by seven-thirty when by rights they should all be mounted before seven) and the older children were schooling two and three horses besides their own. Fences had to be painted, the mares and foals watched with extreme care, and two-year-olds backed sometime soon. It had been lovely, of course, when they'd had no children and only ten horses or so, and nothing really to do, but good Lord, how many hours in the day were there? If he wanted something he could just as well come out and ask for it, rather than making some kind of mystery of it. When she thought about it, she was quite angry. And whose sock was this, stuck in with her underwear? Obviously she would have to talk to him. But, in the end, she shrank from that.

John felt that the proof of his evil nature was complete, but somehow, though it frightened him, it did not depress him. In the mornings he woke up pleased with the 6 A.M. breeze and the leafy treetops against the adamantine blue sky, and during the days he giggled at everything: mother eating carrot strips with a fork, the broad handlebars of Henry's bicycle, Jeepers's sneaky nips at the goslings; even Teddy's evident exasperation with all the accouterments of riding schools rather amused him. He was truly bad; he had become everything that he had always been warned against—callous, deceitful, selfish, thoughtless, sneaky, cruel—and though the thought of one of those words made him gasp when it came to him suddenly, at least it was a relief to know. The perimeters of his future seemed more predictable and therefore more manageable. He was also able to engage Teddy more successfully.

His volts were circular both clockwise and counter; his corners, on the other hand, were as square as could be. At the center of figure eights, Teddy walked his few paces, then took the other lead, whichever one John might desire. His extended trot, though hardly dashing, was competent. His collected trot was best: Teddy's own surprise at the effort he was putting out appeared as style, uncharacteristic lightness. And he had taken again to jumping. Brick walls, oxers, trekehners, triple in-and-outs painted with garish targets, striped poles, solid poles, crossed poles—Teddy charged over everything in his old style, folding his legs and exerting no more effort than necessary. "Perfect working hunter," said mother, self-congratulatory. He forgave his mother. It seemed that someone like himself should forgive everyone.

The Teddy problem he solved himself, shortly after the death of the foal, by relinquishing fifteen years of equestrian training. When he wanted something he gave Teddy a spirited thump, preferably where it would hurt the most. No shyness, striving

131

after tact, or fear of damaging the animal with roughness. Trot NOW! Whap! Stop NOW! Jerk! It was brutal, satisfying, and effective. Though he ached to have tried it out at the canceled show, he was otherwise calm about everything with the equanimity of perfect self-knowledge.

They set out on their weekly circuit of the outside course. One by one the riders galloped from jump to jump, with mother shading her eyes, watching what she could from the top of the Irish Bank. The others were trepidatious; once a week they were set free, with nothing to stop chaotic galloping except barbed wire or electric fencing, with nothing between them and the trees (so close together, with such low branches and rough bark). The creek banks too, slides and precipices. The ever possible fall, and loss of the reins, then of the horse itself. A loose horse, tangled in its reins, falling down and breaking something permanent. These horses would do it, too. But John was exhilarated. He took the course fast, more recklessly than it appeared from mother's distant vantage point. At the slightest notion of hesitation from his mount, he held him in and whipped him over the obstacles. Teddy came home heaving, and mother was surprised at how out of shape he was for this late in the summer. "But resistance," she said, "is turning your energy against yourself, and it never works. Teddy is just one case in point." John giggled. She went on. "If you can really ride, if you can understand the wordless partner and make him into an ally, then you have understood something very pertinent about life itself. And I mean understood it not simply with your intellect, for the intellect of itself is rather feckless, but with your heart and body."

"You're right, mother." Kate gave him a smile of ignorant smugness, and he felt profoundly out of her power, lost already, lost at last.

At noon he cleaned his assigned stalls, ate his prescribed lunch of cereal and milk, and later on he rode again, or soaped

132

saddles, or washed the lunch dishes. There was so much work to do that there was endless time to get used to his new condition.

Every night before dinner, he and Peter worked with the two-year-olds. Margaret and Henry did the extra chores while the two brothers ranged the back field in search of the five colts. "Hey," said John.

"I'm right here."

"I see them." In a deeply shaded sycamore copse near the furthest corner of the field, three of the chestnut beauties were eying them skeptically, as if considering the sweetfeed John carried, but also recent rough mysteries that included bars across the tongue and tightness about the ribs. John rattled the feed bucket. "Hey," he said.

"Well?"

"Have you . . . There're the other two."

"Let's take Holly first, then Boots. The others ought to follow them."

"Yeah." He whistled, then flapped the lead line against the bucket in rhythmic enticement. "Hey."

What do you want?" The habit of being quiet around horses was an ingrained one.

"Nothing. You go that way and kind of ease them toward me."

The strategy worked. Sweetfeed was a potent lure, and the colts weren't all that suspicious, having been handled frequently and tactfully since birth. John slipped the halter over Boots, then fed him a handful of grain and molasses. He liked the animal's snuffling breath, the long, youthful whiskers, the eager tongue. Peter did the same with Holly. The others would get theirs at the gate.

"Hey," said John, when they were trudging back toward the barns.

"Hey what? You sound like a broken record."

"Did you ever kiss anyone?"

"You mean like girls?" Peter was seventeen. Kissing girls had not been much within the scope of his activities, or even his thoughts, though he was not averse to taking advantage of a safe, certain, and desirable opportunity. He said, "Sort of."

"What does that mean?"

"Louise Browne used to kiss me sometimes when we were in the barn together."

"Oh, yeah?" John was impressed. Louise Browne's sojourn on the farm as all-round stablehand was four years in the past. "She was old, though."

"Yeah, she was nineteen."

"She kissed you, huh?"

"A bunch of times." Upon consideration, it seemed to Peter that four times could be termed "a bunch."

"What was it like?"

"I don't know. Like a kiss."

"Come on!"

"I don't know!" They were almost to the gate.

"Well, did she put her tongue in your mouth?"

"I don't remember."

"Did you get hard?"

"I guess."

"Well, Jesus Christ!"

"Well, Jesus Christ to you! It was a long time ago! Open the damned gate!" In any other circumstances he might have said, "the stupid gate" or simply "the gate," though in an exasperated tone of voice. Even now, as he cursed, he looked up automatically for Kate. John opened the gate, controlled the unhaltered two-year-olds while Peter led Holly through and tied him, then led Boots through. The conversation resumed after the three loose colts had been put into stalls, and Peter was easing a light saddle onto Holly, whose eyes were white and huge with distrust. "Stand up!" barked Peter to the leaning horse, but he barked unfearsomely, almost crooningly. Holly stretched out his nose and ground his teeth. John was holding the lead line. He said, "Anybody since?"

"I don't know."

"You must know!"

"I suppose at a party or something."

"Don't you care?"

"I don't know."

This John could not imagine. He was only fifteen, and he was coming to care very much. "Everybody cares," he said. "Even the two-year-olds care, for God's sake." Kate believed in gelding her colts late, for the sake of size and vitality. Peter eased the girth tighter, one strap, one hole, at a time. Holly kicked out quickly, daringly. "Stop that!" said Peter, firmly, but there were no blows, only a cessation of progress. "Walk him," he ordered.

"Yessir!" The colt side-stepped and arched his back; the saddle was still novel, and he kept turning his head for a look at it. After three circuits of the paddock, though, he was calm, almost blasé. John fished a piece of apple out of his pocket and palmed it between the horse's lips. They made three more circuits in the opposite direction. Peter came up and tightened the girth two notches. There was anxiety, but no protest. John found another piece of apple. "A nice colt, I think," remarked Peter.

"Sort of weedy in the neck."

"That might fill out."

"I tried to kiss Lisa Campbell at the horse show."

"No luck?"

"Might have, but mom made us go out to dinner when I was supposed to meet her at the barns."

"Yeah, her and Beanie and every other guy at the show."

"I don't think so."

"Good luck."

"She's not so bad."

"Well, she doesn't sell it, anyway."

After they had tacked up Boots, John said, "Can't you really remember what it was like? I bet she didn't even do it."

"Yeah, well, she did. But, Christ, I was Henry's age, what did I know? I mean, it was nice."

Schooling the five two-year-olds took an hour. When they were done, it was past time for dinner. John said, "I think we're retarded." Peter did not answer. "Really," John went on, "some guys are getting laid, you know."

Still Peter said nothing.

"John Murphy for one, and Bill Scavullo."

Peter turned toward the house.

"You're more retarded than I am. She's done it, you know. The whole family might be normal if it wasn't for her!" Then he marveled at how angry he sounded, because he wasn't angry at all, at least not at Peter. He was just curious, just curious. It was surprising the angers that a person in his condition could stumble into.

A moment before waking Margaret knew she was dreaming, and her dream self said to her waking self, "This is important." The words were precise, distinctly spoken in a firm, rather teacherly voice, but her own voice. The alarm went off. It was 4 A.M., still dark, and not unusually Margaret awoke in full awareness of what had to be done. It was not until a few hours later, during the sleepy forty-five-minute trip to the Lyons County Fairgrounds, that she remembered the voice or any of the dream that had occasioned it. Of that she remembered only a single image, a targeted jump with more jumps beyond it (a triple in-and-out, perhaps?), and the sense of herself toppling toward it, though strangely, very strangely, without fear, without the usual feeling of mixed shame, apprehension, and relief that accompanied falling off a horse, even in dreams.

She was, it was true, oddly nervous about this show, as if in the last week or so the floor had dropped out of her equestrian knowledge, and there was nothing except conscious thought and memory preserving her from danger. Mother's old injuries seemed prominent—always the arm was visible; turned slightly in Margaret's direction, or illuminated by a shaft of sunlight, or inconveniently impeding some action or operation. One, of course, did not think of mother as what you might call "handicapped," but strictly, perhaps, she was.

Once they found their stalls, there was more than the usual confusion setting up, because Peter's first class was at nine, and here it was already eight-fifteen, and MacDougal had worked up such a sweat in the van that he had to be walked out, then brushed all over again before he could even be tacked up. And Peter had forgotten his socks, so that he and John had to share a single pair, and they were to ride in the same class twice in the afternoon. Mother was seriously annoyed. Even so, however, Margaret's hearing was preternaturally acute, and all she was hearing was news of injuries and severe falls since the Chicago show. "Broken collarbone," said someone walking by when she was bent over Mac's left hind foot, painting on linseed oil. "Had to be destroyed right there," wafted from the next group of stalls. "Broke its neck." When she stood up and peered over the bars, she didn't recognize the gossipers. But that didn't make the phrase any less of an omen. When they had at last gotten Peter on board and pointed toward the warm-up ring, Henry ran over from the hotdog stand with the information that Beanie Campbell's new pony had rubbed her off on a tree and broken her wrist. "Yeah?" said everyone, mostly indifferent. Margaret patted Peter's boot. "Be careful," she said. Though quizzical, he was not satirical. He nodded.

It continued all day. Everywhere, the grownup riders were limping and stiff from ancient accidents, and the junior riders were either just getting started again after early summer mishaps, or sitting by the sidelines, resigning themselves to weeks and months of plaster casts and slings and the highly visible inconvenience of crutches. Mother's position on her own injuries, reiterated every time the subject came up, was that you couldn't do anything athletic for twenty, thirty, forty years without suffering damage of some sort, could you? Then she would smile, meaning to reassure, and assert that the principles she taught were most importantly safe ones. Here was Margaret, here were Peter and John and Henry, riding their entire lives and intact, one and all. Now, as she readied Herbie for their first class, regular working hunter on the flat, such luck seemed to Margaret as tenuous as rubber bands, stretching and stretching. Herbie was so solid, though, so demonstrably there, that the looming accident seemed to roll away from her toward one of her brothers. Down the row a stall door slammed in the breeze like a shot, an explosion, a car wreck. Margaret jumped, and thought of Peter falling, rolled on, stepped on, splintered. No one really knew the depths of perversity in MacDougal's heart.

These were not things she usually thought of.

The man, whom Margaret did not immediately recognize, was standing in the way when she pushed open Herbie's stall door. His riding clothes, she then noticed with a start and a blush, were custom made, with old wide-pegged breeches and long tops to the boots. "Excuse me," she croaked.

"Huh?" He only slowly came to attention, and did not seem to recognize her at all. She regained her composure.

"I said, 'Excuse me.' "

"Sorry." But he didn't step out of the way. She blushed again that she had thought so often about someone to whom she was entirely unknown. She said, rather irritably, "Can I help you with something?" He was looking curiously at Teddy, who was dozing. She meant, Go away. "Is there something you want?"

"What? No. Oh, no. I seem to have lost my horses, but I see

them over there. Wrong aisle. Pardon me." He smiled that smile which asserted perfect innocence, and demanded a smile as open in return. Like mother's smile, or Peter's. As with mother and Peter, Margaret complied, and as always with them she felt better afterward. One should, she thought, expect to be forgotten.

After her hunter hack class, which was a failure because she felt too precarious to thrust herself forward and claim the judge's attention, she encountered the man in the warm-up ring. He sat astride his handsome dark gray Thoroughbred, who had a wall-eye, she noticed, and he looked far more attentive.

"Yellow," he declared as she went by.

"Excuse me?"

"I said, 'Yellow.' That horse ought to have yellow ribbons instead of red ones, and you should have a yellow rose in your buttonhole." He smiled again. "Or your hair."

"It would fall out and I would look stupid and unkempt." She pushed the frizzled ends around her ears under her velvet cap. "I have enough trouble as it is."

The ringmaster announced a number. "That's me," said the man. "What's your name?"

"Margaret Karlson."

"Aha!" But he rode away without explaining himself, and had a nice round, good enough for second in the green handy hunter class. Margaret, somewhat to her relief, did not see him again that day.

Seven people fell off, five fell with their horses. The ambulance came into the ring twice, neither time for her or either of her brothers. The socks they were sharing (thank God John was wearing his new boots, which, unlike his old pair, didn't have to be tugged and coaxed for fifteen minutes before he could get his feet into them) seemed to be lucky ones. Teddy, though out of the ribbons in the hack class, won the junior hunter over fences with an astonishing burst of style that included pricked ears and smoothly rounded turns. They were also third in the American Horse Shows Association Medal class, beating out a picture-perfect blonde on a picture-perfect chestnut mare who, when she and John had to trade mounts for individual performances, could not by any means induce Teddy to take the left lead during the figure eight, although he had flown through the maneuver for John. The chestnut mare moved as delightfully as she appeared to, and John had a glimpse of life without strategy before returning her. Only his recent bellicose mood helped him welcome Teddy upon *his* return. There was pleasure to be had at re-entering the fray.

Peter did as well, first winning the Medal class on Herbie (mother did not dare risk some defenseless equestrienne encountering MacDougal if the judge asked Peter to trade horses), then taking second in the junior jumper on his regular mount. The fences in the jump-offs neared five feet, higher than Peter had jumped Mac at home, but to all appearances Peter was imperturbable. They lost by a time fault. The expected catastrophe failed to befall, and Margaret need not have squeezed her eyes shut during the last round, need not have anticipated the huge common gasp, the screams, or the groans.

Mother was pleased. She said, "It's not as if you'd won a combined event, of course, but then . . ." After that she drifted away in the direction of colleagues and compliments, and left the children to close things up for the night. Margaret strayed through the aisle where the man kept his horses. Next to the lovely gray was a Welsh pony, evidence, perhaps, of a child. Margaret felt exposed, embarrassed, nasty. When she got back to their row, she snapped at Henry for not filling the water buckets, although it didn't matter.

It was better, she decided the next day, not to relinquish her fears. Worry, after all, had worked splendidly the day before, rather in the manner of an umbrella. While she was rebraiding

Herbie before the first class ("You've got perfectly good red ribbons on that horse already," said mother, but stopped at the drugstore without being asked), she summoned to mind every accident she could remember, and every one she could possibly imagine. Though hardly as pungent as they had been the day before, her thoughts were quite engrossing. She didn't even glance toward the aisle of the gray hunter and the Welsh pony.

She proceeded to the tail, dutifully envisioning MacDougal's dive through innumerable posts and rails, Peter flipping through space, clawing the air, etc. "What are you doing?" said the man. She had wanted him to appear sometime, but here he was, and she wasn't glad. He pronounced "you" in a peculiar way, entirely specific, almost intimate, as if he enjoyed rights that obviated any necessity of using her name.

"I daren't say."

"Now that you've said that, you must."

"I'm braiding yellow ribbons into my horse's tail."

"Anything else?"

Margaret looked at him for the first time, wondering if he remembered her from the Chicago show, or if he was merely being friendly. Today he wore ratcatcher clothes, browns and golds. These, too, were ampler than the current fashion, and not flattering to his dark hair and fair skin. He was, however, not unhandsome. "Yes," but she grimaced, regretting her coquetry.

"Do go on."

It was best to be as businesslike as possible. "I was thinking about my brother crashing a big post and rails, as a matter of fact."

"Does he do that very often?"

"Hasn't ever."

"Is that your brother who rode the feisty bay jumper yesterday?"

She nodded. "I think if I think about all the possible accidents, then none of them will happen."

141

"But some people say if you worry about things, you draw them to yourself." When she glanced at him hard, alarmed, he went on, "Your brother's an excellent horseman. One of the best I've seen."

"Do you think that makes any difference?"

"I certainly hope so."

"But he's only been this good for the last couple of weeks. I mean, he's always been good, but this is the first year he's ridden Mac, and up until about two weeks ago, they didn't get along at all. I guess I'm afraid that the charm will end. Besides, my mother says that if you ride horses long enough you're bound to get hurt."

"Some folks more than others, I should think."

"Well, she says that, too." She wound the rattail of the braid into a secure knot and hid the end in the side pieces. He said, "You're very good at that."

"I've had lots of practice." Still he used that "you." Oddly, though he was entirely friendly, when he used that "you," she could imagine him accusatory. "We've all had lots of practice at all this stuff, and never any accidents, but I'm sort of superstitious lately. You have a nice gray horse. Well, my mother's had some accidents, before we were grown up. On Mac, that's the bay horse."

"Are you grown up now?"

"Well . . ." He was very grown up. She thought of the Welsh pony. It made adulthood rather dangerous. He was most handsome when he smiled, but also when he smiled he made her think that Peter was the handsomer of the two. Peter, now that she came to think of it, was really quite something. "Excuse me," she said, "I've got to . . ."

"Good morning. I'm Katherine Karlson." Hand extended, teeth glittering, mother had adopted her most hunt-ball manner. The man, who had been leaning against the feed rack, stood

142

up and stepped forward. "Harrison Randolph," he declared. "From Virginia, not these parts, I'm sorry to say."

Mother's eyebrows lifted. No doubt, thought a somewhat embarrassed Margaret, she was impressed by the well-known equestrian name. It was oddly disturbing that mother should be impressed by anything. "Only second cousins," said Harrison Randolph, "and distant ones at that."

"But with the hereditary eye for a horse? I was impressed by your gray yesterday. But he can't be very old?"

"Three-year-old."

Words guaranteed to antagonize. Margaret blushed for the man, and for her mother, who never let an occasion pass. And, indeed, Kate's next comment was a provocative "hmmp."

"Excuse me?" He was very polite, very neat. He looked like a man who was familiar with suit racks and clothes brushes and shoe trees. Surely for that reason alone mother would . . . She did not. She had thrust her hands into the pockets of her old tweed jacket, and now she tossed her hair. "Broken down by five," she said. "You forward-seat Virginians haven't a notion of bones and tendons, I must say. The youngest I've ever shown a horse is as a six-year-old, and you can look at the result." She waved her hand toward MacDougal's and Teddy's stalls. "Fifteen, sixteen years old, and sound through. Never a sidebone, ringbone, osselet even. My vet comes to tend to accidents and that's about it."

Margaret coughed. The man was superhumanly courteous; still smiling slightly, head canted to one side, attentive. From Virginia, though, far away. And one couldn't forget about the Welsh pony.

Mother went on. As John would say, mother could be counted on to go on. "You ride very far forward, in fact. I watched you particularly yesterday, and honestly there were times I was almost uneasy. If you lengthened your stirrups and placed your

143

weight more nearly over the horse's center of gravity, you really would be safer, I think. Such a lovely Thoroughbred shouldn't have to run the risk of having his knees broken." She smiled with dazzling, winning certainty, but Margaret could see the man's excellent manners deflect it. "Perhaps you're right," he responded.

"God bless you," said Kate. "Forgive me. Margaret can tell you. My pet theories." The self-deprecation sounded merely formal.

"Your children have benefitted from them."

"They ride safely, and at times they do well, I'll admit. Margaret," her voice was a bit loud, a bit naked.

"Yes, mother?"

"Are you ready for this class you're in? Where are the boys? Have you had any breakfast? Do you know the course? Have the horses been fed, watered?" Needless queries that she wouldn't have made without a Virginian audience. She didn't await the answers. "I must go, I guess. Margaret too. Your jacket is hanging in the van. Really, I must be off."

"It was a pleasure to meet you, Mrs. Karlson."

"Kate. The pleasure was entirely mine, Mr. Randolph. Do join me in the stands, if your schedule allows?"

"I will, thank you."

"Margaret?" but her voice trailed off as she wandered away.

"Must you go?"

"Soon, anyway." She had tacked up, and was now securing strap ends and picking bits of hay from the corners of Herbie's mouth. She lingered, but after all there was nothing more to say. Once anyone had met mother, there was often nothing more to say.

"Goodness," he said.

"She . . ."

"Your mother is a very powerful person."

"I suppose so. She . . ."

"Can I buy you a hotdog after this class?"

Yes. Yes. Yes. She tightened one of the yellow ribbons. "No, please. I've got to help Peter get ready, I think. There's a lot to do. The boys only have one pair of socks."

"Just a hotdog?"

Could anyone deny that smile? It brought so clearly to mind the other undeniable smiles that she loved. "O.K."

"Meet you back here?"

"O.K." She sounded terribly ungracious, she knew, but she was so embarrassed.

"May I give you a leg up?"

"No, thanks. I'll mount in the warm-up ring. I, um, well, thank you."

"Good luck."

"Thank you."

"Don't forget this." He held out her hairnet.

"Oh, yes. Thank you."

"Thank you."

"Thank you." And then she rode like an idiot and made Herbie refuse a simple brush fence. He hadn't refused a brush fence in four years, said mother, what in the world was the matter with her?

John met her at the barn door when she returned from her class. "You've got to help me," he said. "That asshole's rubbed out half his braids, and I can't find the red ribbon anywhere."

"We used it all up."

"Oh, terrific. My class is in twenty-five minutes."

"Just comb him out. He'll be O.K." Her eyes adjusted slowly to the dimness of the barn. Far away at the end of the aisle, the dark figure of Harrison Randolph appeared, paused, waved, then disappeared.

"Everybody's braided at this show. He's got an ugly mane, anyway. Oh *shit!*"

145

"Look! Just calm down, all right? Take the ribbons off Herbie, and I'll help you do the braiding, but I only have five minutes."

"We have to do his tail, too."

"I won't do his tail. You'll just have to comb it out and go without."

"You can't do that. It says in the AHSA manual . . ."

"It's not the Garden, O.K.? Nobody's going to care."

"I care!" But, teeth grinding, John was struggling to control his temper, and Margaret knew he would resign himself. "Who's that guy?" Harrison was approaching with a smile. "He's a friend of mine. We're going to have a hotdog." She glanced at John, but could tell, with relief, that he wasn't as impressed by this arrangement as she was. "He's awful old, isn't he?"

"No. Now hurry. Where's the water?"

"I haven't gotten any yet."

"Margaret?" Harrison spoke in deeply colored Piedmont tones that made of her name one and a half melodious syllables.

"Hey!" said John before she could speak. "Would you mind getting some water? There's a bucket right next to you."

"I'm sorry, I . . ." interrupted Margaret, but before Harrison could respond, John said, "What are you sorry for? The spigot's right there. We're sort of in a hurry, O.K.?"

"John!"

"Well, we are, aren't we? My class is in fifteen minutes!"

In ten they had him mounted up, and he was lengthening his stirrups while Margaret tucked under the last of the now yellow braids. He rode away without thanks, something Margaret wondered if she was noticing only because Harrison was beside her. When she undid the buttons of her jacket, his hands were on the collar immediately, automatically, and when she glanced at his face, his look was entirely unself-conscious. Good manners were simply good manners. They made her uneasy. She folded the jacket over the top railing of Teddy's stall, wondering how her own manners would betray her, and then, stepping back, she

146

stumbled and fell fleetingly against his chest. His hand gripped her elbow. "O.K.?" he asked.

"Yes." She wanted to add "sir." A hotdog could take as much as half an hour. What in the world would she say to this man?

"Are you in school?" he asked as they negotiated the mucky paddock.

"No."

After a moment he said, "Oh," and she realized that he had expected her to elaborate. "I . . ."

"Are you . . ." They spoke at the same time.

"Sorry."

"Excuse me."

"You live at home, then."

"Of course, doesn't everyone?" But then she understood what he had meant, and felt the thorough stupidity of what she was saying.

"Well, I suppose they do!" He chuckled.

Margaret blushed and grew aware of the fringe of damp ringlets around her hairline. How she hated to sweat the way she did, greasily, and with visibly running moisture. She knew that men hated this.

He reached for her arm as she hopped over a puddle.

"I live at our farm. I always have." And I'm a boring person, don't expect anything from me, don't touch my shirt again, it's damp, don't look at my hair or my throat, where I can feel the runnels gather. She pulled her stock tie out of her breeches pocket and touched it to her upper lip.

"My parents had a lovely farm back in the Blue Ridge Mountains when I was growing up. I was born there, in fact, but they sold it when my father died, before my brother and I were old enough to save it."

"Could you get it back?"

"I don't know." It was clear from his tone that he didn't want it back, and she felt that she had missed the point. By then,

147

however, they had reached the concession booth, and what with standing in line, ordering, paying, and looking for a place to sit, or at least to have some shade, any number of minutes, and opportunities for foolishness, were used up. Then they were eating. Now, she thought, was the time to drop catsup on her shirt front, and sure enough, just as she was lifting the end of her hotdog to minimize the danger, a single ruby droplet plopped between her breasts. He looked at it. She saw him look at it, but she also saw him instantaneously flick his eyes away and pretend that he had seen nothing. He did not, thank God, offer her his handkerchief. "I went to Bennett for a semester."

"Didn't you like it?"

"What?"

"Didn't you like it at Bennett?"

Now there was a question, and as he asked it Margaret realized that she had never looked at it that way. When she thought of Bennett, she thought of the farm, because at Bennett, which she could hardly remember, she'd been obsessed with the farm. "Not really. Where did you go to college?"

"Princeton, then UVa. This trip is actually the first time I've been west of Pittsburgh."

"Do you like it?"

He looked straight at her—at her eyes, her recalcitrant ringlets, her mouth, her throat, her spotted blouse, then at her eyes again, and said, "Yes."

Margaret pushed the last of her hotdog into her mouth, then blotted her upper lip again, this time with the napkin he had given her.

"Hey!" It was Henry at her elbow. "What are you guys doing?" He gazed frankly at Harrison, taking in the old-fashioned riding clothes, the evident adulthood, and the apparent affluence.

"Having something to eat," said Margaret, then, to distract him, "Want anything?"

Henry considered the offer seriously, but declined. "I've had

148

everything already today. Nothing's very good. That other show was better."

"Harrison, this is my brother Henry, the human garbage disposal. Henry, this is Harrison Randolph." She felt uncomfortably new in Henry's eyes, as she had the day she left for college and the boys all whistled at her new clothes.

"Are you from Virginia?"

"Washington, D.C., really, but yes."

"My mother was talking about you to Colonel Stanley." Margaret blushed, as if Kate had read her romantic, and until now successfully hidden, imaginings.

"Are you going to sell your horse to us?"

"Henry!"

"Well, mom said he had a big gray three-year-old just the right size and age for Peter."

"I was thinking, actually, of keeping him for myself."

"You got catsup on your shirt." This Henry addressed to Margaret.

"I know. Go away if you're not hungry."

"I didn't say I wasn't hungry."

"Go away anyway."

"I'm bored."

"You should have ridden, then." But she sounded horribly maternal, horribly like Kate, and she didn't go on. Henry lingered, looking at her, then Harrison, then the selection of candy bars near them. At last, however, he drifted away. After a moment, Margaret said, "My mother always wished we could live in Virginia or Maryland. That's where she was from, originally."

"The Midwest is much nicer, I think. Not so built up, fresher."

"I wouldn't know. I like our farm, though. It's very pretty. People think it's not very hilly around these parts, but our farm is quite rolling, with lots of trees."

"I'd like to see it."

"You can, if you stay around for a couple more weeks. We

have a big show at the end of July every year. You should come."

"Would you like me to come?"

"Well, yes." He smiled, as if she had meant it in some special way, and she was so taken aback that she couldn't think of how to show that she hadn't meant it in any way at all. Admission would be two dollars at the gate. They wanted as many visitors as possible. Still, it made her sweat a little more and breathe a little deeply to think that he would come.

Harrison Randolph looked at his watch. "Uh-oh," he said. "Green hack class in twenty minutes. I've got to run. Say." He leaned toward her slightly, and she felt the warmth of his body. "What are you doing this evening?"

"I don't know if my mother wants to go home or not."

"When will you find out?"

"She could decide at the last moment. It depends on who'll be staying around. She doesn't see some people very often."

He rummaged in his breeches pocket. "Here." It was a card with the name of his hotel on it. "I'm staying there, in room 17. I'd like to see you again."

"Oh."

"Really."

"O.K."

"Good." He trotted briskly off, waving to her, and she didn't know whether she was to call him or go to his room. She stood with the card in her hand, looking at the raised name of the hotel, then the hotel's motto in script, the minuscule letters of the hotel's phone number. "Hey!" she yelled. "You mean I should come?" He put his hand behind his ear, then nodded and made a circle of his thumb and forefinger. Perhaps he had heard, "Should I call?" She took out her cotton stock tie and wiped it over her entire face.

"YOU'RE never going to make it in Medal or Maclay classes," said Kate. "You're almost too old, and anyway we can't afford it." Peter nodded, but she wasn't talking to him as much as she was talking to herself. MacDougal rattled his bits. "You'd better walk him around for a minute. You're so blessedly tall!" His ankle and a third of his calf hung below the horse. "O.K., now look." She did not raise her voice. Nevertheless, because of the intimacy of their relationship (ambitious teacher with best student) he understood her perfectly. "You're past the eyes-forward-heels-down stage. You're past most stages, for that matter. You're almost good. I was good once, for a little while, and you're almost good now. What does that horse feel like to you right now?"

"I don't know. Fine, I guess. He's been pretty calm since the show."

"What's he doing?"

"A free walk."

"Is he bending at the poll?"

"No."

"At the croup? Don't look."

"No, I guess not."

"Are his hind legs moving in long strides or short strides?"

"Fairly long, I guess."

"How can he do that, not bend at the croup, and yet achieve long strides?"

"I don't know."

"You've lived in a home filled with books about equine anatomy for seventeen years, and you don't know how things are attached?"

"I guess not."

"Then how do you expect to know what you are doing?"

"I never thought about it."

"Doin' what comes natcherly?"

"I guess."

"No more guessing."

"Yes, ma'am."

"There are great natural riders. Every nerve and muscle in their bodies recognizes its perfect function astride a horse. They take liberties of form, and their horses don't suffer for them. Sometimes they can't make coherent sentences or put their pants on in the morning without holding on to the dresser. Sometimes they can do lots of things better than everyone else. The lucky ones get their growth early, get on the USET when they're fresh out of Pony Club, and ride in every Olympic Games for the next twenty years. More often, I think, they surface and disappear. You know why?"

"No, I guess not."

"Because you can only be dumb for so long. Momentum only takes you so far. After that you need intelligence, or at least thought, so that you can recognize intelligence when it tells you what to do."

"I . . ."

"You are not a great natural rider. For one thing, you're too tall, and for another, you just haven't got it."

"I'm sorry."

"You don't have to apologize. I don't want you to be a great natural rider, I want you to be a great thinking rider. It's boring and distressing to surface and disappear. I also think that you've got to have lots of disappointment at one end or the other. I'd rather you had yours at this end than at the other end."

"Yes, ma'am."

"Those are only thoughts, not instructions."

"O.K."

"Now pick up a nice collected trot and think about what you're feeling from the horse. What's flexed? What's resisting? How are the little flexions related to the big ones? How about the resistances? They're easier to detect."

"Well, I . . ."

"I don't want to hear about it. Just think. Now tell me. Where do you get the signals?"

"Hands. Thighs, I guess. And the small of your back."

"Then why is it so stiff?"

"I don't know."

"Well, don't go limp."

"Sorry."

"That's better. Did you feel his spine smooth out when yours did? You're sitting on his back. When you hurt him, he's going to defend himself against you."

"Yes, ma'am."

"O.K., post." In a moment she went on. "Now listen. You are going to succeed. You're going to be good, and when you are

153

people are going to talk about what a natural you are, what a genius, how it must run in the genes. Are you listening? People don't like smart riders, really. But I'm telling you not to pay attention to all of that stuff. Listen to me, only to me. I know everything about your seat, your hands, the small of your back, even about the way you think when you're on a horse. If you listen to them, they'll make you think that you are something you aren't, that, for instance, you can't make any mistakes because you're such a natural. That's exactly when you'll make mistakes. If you listen to me, you'll avoid all of that, if you listen to them you'll topple into it. Do you understand?"

"Yes, ma'am."

"I want you to read that big anatomy book in the living room. I left it out on the coffee table. I don't care how long it takes you, but I want you to read it all the way through and not read anything else while you're at it. O.K.?"

"O.K."

"Now pick him up and take him over the brush, at exactly the speed you think he needs to clear it."

"Well, I can't do it by myself," said John. His tone of voice was rising with his temper.

"Don't yell at me! It's not my fault they aren't back yet." Margaret had burned the cheese sauce and discovered only three slices of bread in the breadbox. "Goodness!" she exclaimed.

"Shit!" said John.

"It's only been five minutes, or ten at the most. You'll have plenty of time."

"Five two-year-olds, and she expects them to be backed and schooled and groomed and fed and God knows what else between feeding time and dinner!"

"Well, go get them in and start working on them, and Peter'll come out when he's ready."

"I don't feel like it."

"Hmmmp."

"I didn't ask to do this extra work."

"You did too."

"Not by myself."

"Why are you so grouchy? It's not even hot today. Mercy! Go away!"

"I'm not grouchy." But he was, and he went away.

If he climbed the fence of the warm-up ring, he could see them out on the practice field, doing much the same as they had done that morning: sitting trot, posting trot, serpentines, volts, large circles, halts. Instead of ensconcing herself in a chair on the Irish Bank, though, mother was following Peter around, calling to him (once or twice the breeze carried the sound of her voice) and gesticulating occasionally. "Shit!" said John. It was after five. His most efficient course of action was plain: he should find the colts, bring them in (they were quite tractable now that the anticipation of feed was fixed in their imaginations), groom one or two of them, and by that time Peter would be finished and ready to help. The both of them were really only necessary when it came to mounting, which they had been doing for the last three days, and leading. He continued, however, to sit on the fence, watching his mother and his brother, though their actions were too far away to discern.

He was terribly, churningly curious, although not about the details of their lesson. Those he knew without thinking about them; mother's act was one that replayed itself daily. What tantalized him was the nature of their new relationship, and more importantly its significance. He knew with perfect and painful clarity that it was significant, and that it had to do with every note on the bulletin board that ridiculed Peter's form and judgment, with every exasperated sarcasm she had flung at him in front of the others, with every despairing remark she made about the size of his clothes, the expense of keeping him in boots, the ludicrous necessity of buying a new big horse when the place was teeming with horses already. He, John, was the right size (short) and had probably stopped growing. But he, John, was sitting on the fence, and Peter, gangly and stupid, was astride MacDougal, mother's favorite horse, the idol of numerous boring anecdotes. Peter was out there in the field, having extra lessons.

His vision strained after the three figures, and his hearing labored to learn that the sessions were remedial. They were not, though. He knew that. And, in a summer filled with more longing and more anger than he had ever known in his life, he had not yet felt the breathless and constricting anger and longing that he felt now. Peter drew Mac to a nice square halt. Mother put her hands on her hips, spoke, raised one hand to her eyebrows, continued speaking. Peter nodded. At last he turned toward the warm-up ring, walking loosely. Mother followed, still talking.

"Well," she said when she saw John.

He could think of nothing to say that wasn't a demand or a plea, and so he looked at her, mustering as much antagonism as possible, and said nothing.

"Are the two-year-olds in? It's nearly five-thirty."

"No."

"No, what?"

"No, ma'am."

"What have you been thinking of? For heaven's sake, John, you make me very angry. Do I have to watch you and instruct you every second of the day? You're fifteen years old now. I should think . . ." She turned to Peter. "Get that horse put away this instant."

"I was just watching," muttered John.

"You don't have time to watch. You have responsibilities, as you well know. We all do. That's how we can afford, and just barely afford, let me tell you, the privilege of living on a beautiful farm like this. . . ."

"I didn't ask to live here."

"You sound like a fool."

"Well, I didn't."

"'Well, I didn't!' 'Well, I didn't!'" The tone of her mockery was squeaking, strident. "No one, not one of my other children tries my patience like you do. I would have to be a saint to put up with your resentments, your foot-dragging, your evil temper. I'm telling you, I can't stand it anymore!" She was nearly shouting. "Now get down from there and do the task you agreed to do! If you're late for dinner, so much the worse for you. You'll get what's left over!"

"Why are you yelling at me?" Now it was his turn to shout. "I was just watching! I might as well watch, since I'm not going to get to do any of that stuff—never ride MacDougal, or any other decent horse, never get an extra lesson, never get a chance to win anything. That's right, I'll get what's left over, after he's finished with what he wants. It's O.K., though, you just do what you're planning. You just ship me off to college and get me out of here. That's exactly what you'd like to do, and since you do everything you want to do and nothing anybody else wants to do, that's what you'll do. I'm as good as he is, you know. Every bit as good, and a lot smarter, and a lot shorter too, for that matter."

"Then prove it."

"Maybe I don't want to."

"You act like a five-year-old. You expect me to hand you everything on a silver platter, and when you don't get it, you stamp your little foot and cry. All you can say is 'me! me! me!' Well, I'm tired of it. When you've proven to me that you're ready for extra experience, then you'll get it. Right now all you've shown is that you can't even do what's expected of you so far." She paused, then suddenly thinking of herself arguing with him,

157

a child, she flamed up more fiercely. "I can't stand it! Get out of my sight! Do your work! I can't bear to speak to you!" Her usually strong voice cracked with effort and anger. "Go away!" she choked. He did so. Even this full of hatred, violent, spitting hatred, he feared her granite-chip eyes.

Her anger was huge, filling the dinner table, the kitchen, the house, annihilating the peace of the entire farm. She said nothing, although the cheese sauce tasted burnt and the children had biscuits instead of bread, and Henry complained that he couldn't eat his dinner. Her anger was so enormous that Henry's petulance could not increase it. It seemed, especially to her, monolithic, grotesquely permanent; the place itself seemed fixed in time now: the dinner dishes would never be done, or even cleared from the table, the pantry door would never close upon onions and potatoes that would never sprout or decay, the arrangement of the boots in the corner boot pile was immutable, the selection of notes on the bulletin board a historical artifact. Soon the family would leave the dinner table and vanish, as the charred bodies had vanished from Pompeii. There was the muted requesting of this and that, there were muted thanks and apologies. Kate sat wordless and did not eat. She would, it seemed, sit and sit and sit. When the children had eaten every morsel and drunk every drop on the table, they sat as well. No instructions about the dishes or other after-dinner chores were forthcoming.

At last Axel said, "I went to see my sweetheart, she met me at the door, her shoes and stockings in her hand, her feet all over the floor."

"Oh, daddy!" whispered Margaret, but she covered one bare foot with the other anyway, and pushed both as far as possible under her chair. "I never go outside without them," she said.

"Disaster could strike at any moment, and then where would you be?"

Kate scowled. Things were veering in the direction of levity. The spell of perpetuity was broken, for one thing. In a moment, in a very short moment, she knew that they would cease to take her seriously. They would shrug, say to themselves that she would get over it eventually, and go about their business. Business of some kind, probably the wrong business, and so, soon, she would have to speak. More than anything she could not bear the thought of speaking. She said, "Henry! Dishes."

"No," said Axel.

"Pardon me?"

"No. You and I are going to do the dishes. The children can have the evening off, as long as they clear out of the house."

"There's plenty to do around here. . . ."

"The master has spoken." He smiled. The role was so unusual for him that the children stared. The spell was indeed broken, simply because there was something of more interest than mother's anger, after all. They cleared out. The pantry door slammed shut, the boot pile diminished, and, in a moment, children's voices were to be heard from a distance. In a way, it seemed to Kate a miracle, at least as much of one as all those she was every day declaring to be miracles.

He did not settle into his chair, plant his elbows beside his plate, and impale her with a monitory gaze. Nor did he seek forgiveness for contradicting her before the children. Instead, he smiled, dropped a fork, picked it up, began gathering together the plates, pushed the butter dish toward her so that she would put it away, stood up humming and turned his back to her.

"I don't appreciate . . ." she began.

He turned the water on full blast.

When the sink was full and steaming, he closed the taps and said, "Do you remember when Margaret was three and we sent her to nursery school, and they asked her what her name was, and she told them all it was 'Sweetheart'?"

Kate could see everything very clearly, and in the first place, since she was the least sentimental person she had ever met, nostalgic references to quaint incidents of their mutual past were not going to soften her up. In the second place, and more importantly, no one knew her husband's tricks better than she did: the devious nonreference that would eventually lead around to the main subject, the comradely smiles, just slightly self-deprecating, that were meant to induce trust in the victim, the sudden offers to buy something or do something inserted smack in the middle of the argument, which were at least intended to distract one from the point, and at worst intended to bribe. At one time there had been a whole category of ploys involving the touching of her cheek, or the arm about her waist. Innocent, but still cajolery. She pursed her lips. Once he had perfected a whole routine of horrifying but harmless pratfalls, and had teased her into good humor with them for nearly a year. Then they had stopped. One had to admit that he knew to the moment when repetition ceased to be funny and started to be contemptible. She said, "Hmmp."

"Bob Baron came into my office today and said that his granddaughter had announced to her day-care group that her name was 'Shithead.'"

"I don't like that kind of talk."

"Neither did Bob. He was rather horrified, really. He kept saying, 'Karlson, why did she marry that idiot?' I didn't know what to say. Hand me those glasses, would you?"

Kate wiped the table with short, resentful strokes, on the verge of denouncing this enforced domestic togetherness. To coordinate their actions, to make a minuet of this household task that Henry should be doing, all in the name of something that no longer existed between them, was an abomination.

He grinned. "I had to laugh when he left, though. It is pretty funny." His grin indicated that fools like himself would laugh at anything. His grin indicated that four children, forty horses, three hundred acres, and an angry wife hadn't yet encumbered his sense of humor.

Kate turned her back on him, ostensibly to straighten the pantry shelves. Behind the soup cans, there were onions that had rotted into the wood. "Yecch," she said, in spite of herself.

"What's the matter?" He was at her side instantly.

"Look."

"I'll clean it up, don't worry about it."

This she should not fall for. This, especially since not five minutes before she had foreseen something of the kind, she should set her face against. There was something so repellent about rotten food, though, that she was grateful in spite of herself. In spite of herself, she said, "When I was little I used to think that this was where snakes came from." Then it seemed bitter to have allowed him that intimate detail. "I was only four." And now she was in deeper. He bumped against her. It was intentional.

"Excuse me," he said, before she could tell him not to do that, and then he was back at the sink, commendably scrubbing away at the burned cheese sauce. He dared to hum. How could he be so puerile, so playful, so adept at invading her? She wanted to scream about how hard she had worked to make their partnership as smooth and impersonal as it was, how hard she had plotted to maximize everyone's freedom within the limits of a single family, a single homestead. She wanted to reassert, to nail it into permanent understanding, that no incursions were allowed for or permitted. Life must go on as it had. Who knew what would happen if they tried something new? She wanted to say, "This is not what I want."

Nothing, however, could be said. He held up the saucepan, now rinsed and spotless, for her praise. It would be impossible to convince a third party that this was a terribly significant act, insisting upon attention from her that it was a betrayal of herself to give, yet she knew it was. "Oh, good," she said, as if the vessel had been found mysteriously scoured early one morning. She found the broom and swept, hoping to concentrate and ignore. He continued to hum, and Henry burst in, slamming the back door. "Out," said Axel.

"I'm hungry."

"You had your chance." He spoke before she could, saying the words that were on her tongue. It was not significant.

"Mom, I'm hungry."

It galled her to cooperate. The united front they had heretofore presented joined at an abutment. There had been no overlap in years. "Out," she might say, or "Listen to your father," or "Have a peanut butter sandwich," but every utterance she could think of involved the breaking of one rule or another, one custom or another. How could it be so easy for him to destroy her hard-won system? To say nothing was not her way, either. Saying nothing felt like a relinquishing of her due authority. "You're always hungry," she said.

"But now I'm especially hungry. Now I'm really and truly hungry."

"Go on," she said. "Go outside." There it was, the worst possible kind of weak, wifely support. And it left them alone together. She wanted to scream.

She swept, he wiped. For a long angry second she beheld with liquid clarity the tableau of the last ten years. Each family member had been like a runner in a lane, moving forward, struggling in solitude with the effort and the pleasure, learning, with each stride, to know him or herself a tad, a point, a dash better. Kate loved the white lines of the track, the way they defined it, guided and limited the runners, and yet were merely lines, not fences, not walls. A foot could not cross the lines, no interference could occur, but a hand could reach out, support or even hold another hand, briefly. All because of the lines. Their family had lived a life described by more rules than the lives of many families: stable management rules, equestrian rules, rules about household duties and schoolwork, religious guidelines and dictates on the subject of good manners, as well as the private code of Kate's and Axel's marital relations. Kate felt certain in herself of the loveliness of those rules, of the difficulty and the nearly sensual pleasure in following them, in, indeed, lashing oneself to them. She wanted to say to Axel, "Don't think it hasn't been hard," but that would be a non-sequitur and, worse, a plea.

She wanted to say, "These children write thank-you notes, these horses are well cared for, we have what we want," but she couldn't speak, and Axel resumed his humming.

When he had rinsed and wrung the sponge, placed it neatly on the rear left corner of the sink, then he turned, smiling, and she stood still with the broom in her hand. "Well!" he said. What would happen to the runners now, after ten years on the track? The vision did not fade, but in his hearty "Well!" she knew that it lost its relationship to reality. The terrain changed. There would be no lines anymore.

"Honestly," she said, "John makes me so angry!"

"He always has."

"Oh, really!" She wedged as much contempt as possible into her tone.

"He always has. He's like your father."

"Nonsense." It was she, they'd always said, who was like her father. "I don't believe in all this family resemblance rigmarole."

"The horse breeder speaks." He grasped her arm above the elbow. He could, it appeared, do anything now. First a shoe on the floor of her room, and then the wrenching of her arm. "Katherine!" he said. "Why don't you forgive . . ."

"I always forgive him! and then he always angers me again."

"Us?"

"Pardon me?"

He did not, however, repeat himself. Nor was he any longer gripping her arm. He was, in fact, walking away from her into the living room, the living room with its two other doors and the big French window, with its many distractions, the living room like a sieve. She hurried after him, but between the living room and the front hall she lost him.

"What if you had some leftover fried chicken," said Henry. "How long would that last if you were away from the refrigerator?"

"What?" This was the third of Henry's questions, though she was ostentatiously paying little attention, and Margaret began to get annoyed with his persistence.

"How long would leftover fried chicken last outside the refrigerator?"

"I don't know. A day, maybe. I'd like to read this, if you don't mind."

"I don't mind."

Margaret turned back a page and reread the paragraph she had missed. The book was called *How to Be Your Own Best Friend*.

"What would last the longest?"

"I'm reading!"

"Just answer this one question."

"Cereal, I suppose. Crackers. Maybe beef jerky or something like that."

"Oh." Henry got to his feet, and, drawing his fingertips over the backs of mother's books reflectively, left the room. In a moment he was back. "Do you have the two dollars I lent you?"

"If I give it to you right now, will you leave me alone for the rest of the evening?"

"Yeah."

"Look in the top left-hand drawer of my desk."

"Thanks."

"You're *welcome!*" But when he had finally gone, Margaret dropped the book in her lap and rested her gaze on the stack of magazines across the room. They were copies of *The Chronicle of the Horse,* and she knew that if she thumbed through them or through numbers from previous years, she would find mention of Harrison Randolph and his horses. And it would be nice simply to read his name and to know the names of his various mounts.

She had not, in the end, either called him or gone to his room (as if she could have gone to his room!) on the last night of the horse show, even though mother's decision to have dinner with friends from Indiana and to leave the following morning had given Margaret a few hours to herself. During Kate's absence she had done an odd thing: After brushing off her riding clothes and cleaning her boots, which she tried to do at the end of every show, she had taken a long hot bath, washed her hair, and scrubbed her body very carefully. She had cleaned under her fingernails, twirled the wax out of her ears with a Q-Tip, rinsed off under the shower, then rubbed some of mother's hand cream into her skin. She even used a nail file on the calluses of her feet. Then she brushed her hair dry, dressed in her last clean blouse and best slacks, and went for a walk around the motel, though only to the lobby, where she bought a package of Life Savers. Immediately she returned to her room, taken off her fresh clothes, and gotten into her nightgown, turned on the television, and climbed into bed. What was odd, besides her unaccustomed thoroughness, was that she thought happily of Harrison Randolph the entire time, felt almost as if she were preparing for a date with him, except somehow, since she wouldn't be seeing him, the pleasure of the preparations and the affection of her thoughts weren't damaged by anxiety. It was enough, at the time, that he wanted to see her again, and that when she went to the lobby of her motel she was fit to be seen. Anything more would have destroyed her equilibrium.

She had, of course, been silly. In retrospect (and there had been plenty of retrospect) she knew that, but when she thought back to the pure, solitary sense she had had of simply being clean and desirable as she flipped through the *New Yorker*s and *Times* on the magazine stand and compared that to the self-disgust she had felt in his presence (as a result of his presence?), she was satisfied. But now she wanted to scour old *Chronicle*s for his name and the names of his horses, to imagine him in his old-fashioned riding clothes guiding impeccable Tidewater steeds over rich, sturdy courses: over brush fences that grew green where they were standing, trimmed like topiary every season, over ditches and rails and chicken coops lit by the wealthy sun of lifelong hunt-club subscriptions, over . . .

She pursed her lips and cut her fantasy off short. Who knew better than she the true nature of a horse show, the nastiness of the people, the wastefulness of the expense? She picked up her book. He had very nice hands, though. She could picture them perfectly, and she didn't even remember noticing them.

"You only had a five. Here's your change." The bills Henry handed her were flat and smooth. He had too much respect for money to wad it up the way John and Peter did, or to stuff it, uncounted, into a pocket. He kept it neatly in the top drawer of his dresser, and he had seventy-three dollars and thirty-four cents. Now, besides mother, the only person who owed him anything was John, five dollars. Mother's debt was a dime she had borrowed for the mailman, and he didn't expect to get that back, though it was hard to stop thinking about it.

Henry had fixed his final plan. On the second day of the family horse show, a day of the utmost conceivable chaos, he would gather up his provisions, pack his raincoat, and pedal away.

Casual requests, which had been sufficient with Peter and Margaret, had no effect on John, who said that if Henry made a pest of himself he would get pounded, because some people had a lot of things to do before the horse show. Henry recognized the validity of this argument in terms of their fraternal relationship and the weight and height John had over him, but he was nonetheless determined, the next morning, to risk the pounding and chance the repayment.

"I want my money," he said, when they went first thing to bring in the geldings. This he had not said for two days, so he figured it was safe to be direct.

"You do, huh?"

"Yes. You said you'd give it back as soon as we got home from the show."

"Is that what I said?"

"Yeah."

"Didn't you ever learn not to pay attention to what I say?"

There was no answer to this, so Henry reiterated, "I want my money." Then, after a pause, "It's my money."

"There they are. You go around that way." The geldings had stationed themselves in the woods overlooking the creek, deep in shade and still cool. There had been no rain in about two weeks. Henry circled around behind the animals; they were not as gullible as the two-year-olds, and lately had had to be chased in. "Hyah!" he shouted. Heads jerked up, more annoyed than surprised. Through the trees came John's yell. "Git! You, too, Snip." One or two started trotting. *"Hyah! Hyah!"* shouted Henry, laying his lead rope across Mr. Sandman's flanks without a flutter of nostalgia. The remarkable self-sufficiency of the bicycle, which had neither to be fed nor entered in competitions had entirely removed Mr. Sandman from his heart.

The way John looked, twenty yards away, short, wiry, dark, and almost muscular, was the way Henry would look in three years. The clothes John was wearing, in fact, Henry would be wearing himself someday, except that he was about to take himself out of the hand-me-down rankings. John's strides were short and his mannerisms energetic. These would be Henry's too, with modifications in the direction of carefulness and conservation of effort. Everything that had been John's became Henry's, and he didn't mind. Sometimes, when he thought about John and about his imminent departure, it seemed as if he would continue to live here after all, as much of him as was necessary.

"You're going to go in the family class, aren't you?" said John, when they were walking in behind the geldings. The family class took place toward the end of the second day. Though of course they had never won (mother had an agreement with the judge), the Karlsons had ridden in the family class every year since the first show, when Henry was two and rode on the pommel of mother's saddle. He had forgotten. When he hesitated, suddenly panicked about his plan, John went on, "Shit, even dad goes in the family class." It was true. Every year father got out his woolen breeches and brushed off his old coat and walked, trotted, and cantered around the ring with the rest of them.

"Sure."

"She's not going to make you pay an entry fee, tightwad."

"I know. Say, speaking of that . . ."

"There's Lucky heading for the creek. You'd better get him while I drive the rest of them in."

"You get him." But this was perfunctory, uttered in the very act of pursuit. He mostly, after all, did what John said.

He came to the warm-up ring just as John was mounting up; his shout, intended to preface a demand for payment at lunchtime, went unheeded. He went and found his bicycle.

It was midsummer hot, but he was industrious in his pedaling, squinting his eyes against the glare and wrinkling his nose against the dust. His body had changed in the last month. Muscles were more visible, and veins spread angular and soft, like gopher tunnels over his forearms. The thought of leaving did not please him although it did not exactly frighten him, either. For the most part, he could imagine nothing beyond bicycling down the road, and that he had done enough now not to thrill to it. He was apprehensive of large dogs, lightning, and groups of jeering older boys, but not of solitude, distance, or

168

running out of money (people, he assumed, would be quite willing to give money to a twelve-year-old boy in return for less work than his mother got for free). Separation from the family did not intimidate him, and from this he divined that he must not like them very much. He was confident that he could manufacture a convincing story if he had to, and that the story would arise out of the demand itself, a perfect flower of a story, complete, credible, having even a bit of grace.

He pedaled up the two hills and coasted down, not too preoccupied with the future to fail to enjoy the exhilaration and danger of the small bridge. Just as he had never been anxious about Christmas or his birthday or the end of school, just as he had awaited those days with equanimity and greeted them with a quiet sense of achievement, now he was not anxious about his new life. He expected to become, eventually, rich, powerful, and grown-up. He expected to eat many delicious meals. He expected to begin upon these accomplishments very soon, since, as he knew what he wanted, there was no reason to delay. He expected to remain single-minded, calm, and detached for the rest of his life. He expected the mainspring of the farm to tick forever, and to measure his days to those regular ticks, which he expected never to lose the sense of. To anticipate that morning, four days hence, to get excited, to smile to himself, to lie awake, would jeopardize the inevitability of everything, and so he pedaled and coasted, and pedaled some more, and at lunchtime went home for his usual peanut butter sandwich. While he was dipping up the grape jelly, John banged into the kitchen, and it came to Henry that he was going to neither speak of nor expect the money, that this decision was irreversible, and that there was something about his relationship with John which he did not now understand but one day would.

BESIDES riding, they recovered, then painted and repaired all the jump poles and standards on the farm. New ones were ordered from the lumber yard and delivered, as well as three new panels and a new chicken coop. Kate closed her eyes at the expense. The scattered logs of many log jumps on the outside course were gathered together and stacked imposingly. The brush jumps were newly filled with brush, old hay-bale jumps remade with fresh, square bales. Oddities were contrived. Father got out the tractor and pulled a huge log into place over a trail through the woods. John and Peter tacked together an old five-barred gate. Louis came back to the farm for two days to mow all the pastures to a prosperous yellow-green. Two cracked panes of glass in the main barn were repaired, and Axel, in an extravagant mood, replaced the baling-twine gate fasteners with chains and hooks. Pony Clubbers came to brush and braid their mounts three days in advance, just so the braids would fall out and they could do it again. Saddles were soaped, saddle blankets taken to the laundromat in town and put in the heavy-duty machines. The dishes were left undone, the beds unmade, the family's underwear unwashed.

John and Peter shoveled out the visitors' stalls and planned where they would hide the family tools so that strangers wouldn't carry them away. The scoreboard for the combined event was whitewashed, the lines redrawn. The judge's tent was rented (this year green and white) and chairs were found and tables and pads of paper and extension cords. Pony Club mothers agreed to take care of refreshments, fought over the inclusion of diet soda pop, decided in favor of popularity over nutritional value, and sent their husbands over with great tubs for ice. The man with equipment for hotdogs and hamburgers appeared, set up the equipment, and left. Three Pony Club mothers and seven Pony Club siblings wrapped a thousand cheese sandwiches, all with mustard, none with mayonnaise. The screen door banged continually. Mother was everywhere, as calm as possible, having no effect on the chaos.

Riders continued their daily lessons, now beginning at seven, to leave more time for preparations. As the show approached, the show in which *they* were to compete, the Pony Clubbers became insensibly overawed with Peter. They spoke always about how good he really was, how the judge, a retired member of the Team, was really coming to see Peter in action more than anything else. It was felt privately that this man of wisdom might pick one of them out of the crowd as well, see nascent genius among the beginners as only fresh, unprejudiced eyes could do.

Expectations of the man's infallible wisdom rose and rose as Peter's private lessons with his mother lengthened. Obviously she was grooming him for something. John was not the only one who casually strained his sight in their direction as he went about

171

his chores, nor the only one whose every encounter with Peter was fraught with unasked questions about what mother had said, promised, and prophesied. To John it seemed that there must have been some note to this judge, some postscript instructing that he look especially closely at mother's oldest son, and he ground his teeth at the thought. He imagined a tunnel vision that would inexorably exclude his own claims for notice. He felt it had been unfair of mother to prejudice the observer before he even came, before he had a chance to look around and draw his own conclusions. If anything, he felt, Peter ought to have been handicapped somehow, since he had the flashiest horse. The judge would certainly notice Peter. The person he should be encouraged to notice was John himself, who was doing excellent things with an indisputably second-rate mount.

Peter, whose focus had narrowed considerably, almost totally, saw nothing but MacDougal; Mac he saw with a depth of field that was exhaustive and crystal clear. He had come to function as the perfect pivot point between the voice of his mother and the energies of his horse. Twenty-one hours a day he seemed about normal. He did his share of the work and the joking and the squabbling. He flirted absent-mindedly with the girls, giving the usual impression that he wasn't aware of flirting, and therefore having great success. But his mind, more than ever, was on something else (and his mind had dwelt on many other things than the business at hand for as long as anyone could remember). It was on MacDougal.

During riding class he had usually, at least more than any other time, paid attention. Now, however, his attention was ferocious and continual and inarticulate; he could not be said to be thinking about riding, if "thinking" was to imply something to do with words. Although he read the anatomy book and memorized the terms, although he read the other books mother assigned him, and then answered her questions when she quizzed him during their afternoons together, and although her endless flow of talk was as the air itself, he understood nothing in terms of words and everything in terms of the way his bones and muscles and eyes and hands encountered the horse.

"Think of the cannon bone," said Kate. He was trotting around the warm-up ring. He thought of the cannon bone—straight from knee to ankle, simple, solid, guyed with ligaments and tendons. "What is the cannon bone doing now?" said Kate. "And what is the cannon bone doing now?" (He halted, he cantered forward, he took a small fence. MacDougal's four cannon bones flashed rhythmically and dependably in the sunlight.) And the cannon bone was by far the simplest of them all. The hoof, for example, was enough to boggle the mind. He hardly heard her questions, hardly heard his own answers, but their effect was to etch the drawings he had looked at into his memory, and further, to endow them with movement and meaning. These days MacDougal amazed him.

Success, compared to this—that is, the success of blue ribbons and praise from ex-members of the Team—was laughably irrelevant, and yet to all appearances he was bent on exactly that sort of success, and it was clear even to him that it would be forthcoming.

To John it was even clearer. Teddy groaned and farted and schemed for snatches of grass that showed green at the corners of his bits, looking untidy. He rubbed his enormous head against fenceposts and passersby, pulling strap ends out of their keepers and disarranging his bridle. He closed his eyes, hung his head, and resembled a plow horse. He rubbed John's careful braid out of his tail, breaking the hairs and making it impossible to rebraid. Everything that was done had to be done over. Nothing that was done enhanced Teddy's looks, and so nothing that was done brought esthetic pleasure. John smacked him with his hand, berated him, vented upon him the full force of his exasperation. Astride he had formed the habit of covert but abandoned vehemence, and it was an intoxicating habit.

During every lesson, John's turn came right after Peter's. In every group movement, he was to keep his eyes on MacDougal's beautiful hindquarters and silky tail, to keep his distance, but not to lag behind. After Peter galloped over a short jump course in perfect style and balance, he was to do the same. It was clear he could not hope to do better. How, he thought, had Peter, who had been just another of them two months before, grown so fair and golden, so graceful and precise, in a mere number of days? How did days add up in this way?

John spurred Teddy and held him in. The horse arched his neck and approached for a moment the condition of having flair. The horse lagged. If mother wasn't looking, John fluttered his whip, a proscribed behavior because it made horses whip shy, and, eventually, insensitive; the horse perked up. Peter made no mistakes. He held his hands low and quiet. He indicated gait and directional changes by a shift of weight. The small of his back, always within John's purview, flexed like a bow. His shoulders floated, his neck floated, his chin floated, his horse floated. His hair ruffled in the breeze, he was fair and beautiful. John had only two choices: to love his brother and hate himself, or to hate his brother and love himself. Mother shouted at him to pay attention, for goodness' sake, he was sticking his chin out from here to Buffalo. He realigned himself with a start, and Kate considered, with pardonable pride, that her judgment about Teddy had been just right. John was definitely shaping up, yes indeed. She smiled. He hadn't grown a centimeter since Christmas, either.

Everything, fortunately, had gone wrong. Kate was at her very best. From insufficient extension cords for the announcer's stand to questionable mayonnaise on a hundred and twenty-four tunafish sandwiches (Henry, who had sneaked the hundred and twenty-fifth, was being watched carefully for symptoms. He told everyone he encountered that it had tasted all right to him). Kate

174

was commanding, shining with hospitality, as manly as a cavalry officer in her pressed shorts and crisp madras shirt. Like everyone else, Axel wished to follow her around, asking for orders and reassurance. Pony Club mothers and fathers, in feed caps, bermudas, and short-sleeved shirts, were being greeted and blessed continually, whether they brought station-wagons full of cold lemonade or only themselves and their bright-faced daughters. Kate alone blazed with the capacity to bring order to everything, and even Axel was prey to the twenty-year illusion, although it was he who knew where the extension cords should be, and he who ordered the sandwiches thrown out, correctly estimating the cost of even the slightest risk.

This was hardly the first show he had stayed home to help with, but it was the first to move more than his sense of duty. Usually, crowds of people roaming the farm offended him. They did not so much endanger things (fences, equipment, livestock, themselves) as they violated the place and weighed it down. Every year after the horse show, there was more dust and less greenery, the lingering odor of automobile exhaust and the belongings of strangers (women's underwear was the most offensive). When objects of value were lost (every year someone's watch, someone's paycheck), the item in his imagination seemed to erode the ground it lay on, and he was unwontedly angry, as well as assiduous in directing the search.

This summer, however, the inconveniences of the horse show were secondary when he thought of them at all. What he anticipated was the fascination of watching his wife for three days straight, of catching her eye, of paying sudden attentions to her that would make her mispronounce a word or blush or forget who had just spoken to her. His flirtation of late had gone so well that he was wildly curious to pursue it, the more so because in her way she was pursuing it too. When she looked at him, he saw what he expected in her face: recognition, curiosity, and the resigned dread of a child diving off the high board. He

175

exulted and pretended to see nothing, waiting within the shell of their customary relationship for her to get fed up or bored or anxious, waiting for some impatience that he could turn to his own advantage. He suspected that the chaos of the horse show might bring it about. He knew that, in spite of her crisp shorts and spruce shirt, her effusive attention to riders and parents and potential customers, it was him she was thinking of.

She was standing in the way of the doodad drawer in the kitchen, where they kept string and toggle bolts and extension cords. "Excuse me," said Axel.

"Yes?" She looked up beaming, expectant. Probably, he thought automatically, taking him for a child or some Pony Club father.

"I need to get in there." He motioned at the drawer.

"Oh, really! Of course! Let me get out of the way." She continued to smile and failed to move.

"Well, get out of the way." At his smile they were embarrassed, and she went back to writing her note while he rummaged for a fourpenny nail. He found it, looked for another one, noticed that she had started to doodle on the note. Now she wadded it up and wrote again, but still it was difficult, impossible, to speak.

"I want Henry to keep Talbot and the announcer supplied with cold drinks," she said. "He isn't riding, after all."

"It does seem like it's going to be very hot."

"Yes, indeed."

"I thought that I'd nail that sagging shutter up temporarily. After the show I can get a hinge. They're pretty old." At the beginning of their marriage, they had traded similar information in similar, almost false-sounding tones; these were not false, though, rather the efforts of two people whose lifelong refuge had been good manners to take refuge again. He smiled at the thought. He felt not victorious but happy.

"Mrs. Karlson!" wailed a Pony Clubber from the doorway,

176

"Phoebe took Snip out of his stall and gave him a whole bunch of water, and my class is supposed to start in fifteen minutes, and he'll get sick!"

"What class is it, Sidney?" She knelt beside the girl and put her arm over the small shoulders, an unwonted gesture that surprised and gratified Axel, since he knew that it was for him.

"Walk-trot."

Kate stifled a smile. "We'll watch him, sweetheart. But I think he'll be fine."

"She shouldn't have done it."

"I know." Suddenly Kate stood up, glanced at him. Curiosity, fear. She had recollected herself. She followed the child outside, and in a moment he could hear her voice raised in the old, commanding tones.

It seemed to Margaret that if she lodged a few very specific things in her mind, then a few very specific others would not have room to enter. Getting the smaller Pony Clubbers on their horses without temper or tears was one thing, keeping their mothers and fathers out of the way was another. "Thank you," she would say, "but of course we try to make them as self-sufficient as possible. It really is safer that way. Yes, the horse is very big, but one of the gentlest on the farm, believe me." She repeated it over and over, walking the parent away from child and horse. Then there were the farm tools to keep track of. Each pitchfork and shovel and rake was painted with a bright yellow stripe around the handle, and she sighed each time she noted a striped handle in the hands of a stranger. She also glanced into vans and trailers and collected the striped handles that she found. The feed room, fortunately, had been padlocked, and here was something else to think of—the whereabouts of the key.

In addition, of course, were her classes (four plus the combined event) and Peter's (it would be awful if Talbot Light didn't even notice, and worse if he sneered). One could also think of John's classes (he deserved something after a summer on Teddy) and wonder whether Henry would ride in the family class and try to figure out where that package of three hairnets had gotten to, and concentrate on every little thing, even the way one's boots looked as one walked to the hotdog stand, but still there seemed to be both time and energy left over for the inspection of license plates, sight and thought left over to survey the crowd of riders and horses, even spectators, for a face and body she knew she would recognize the instant she saw it.

There were no Virginia license plates, no gray three-year-old Thoroughbreds, not even any certifiable Welsh ponies, and the only old-fashioned breeches around belonged to Lambert Smith, seventy-three years old, who did mother the favor of riding in her horse show every year on the same questionably sound dun cob that he had hunted in the Cotswolds and in the Maryland Hunt country in better days. "Bless you," said Margaret. "Mr. Smith, we can always count on you!"

"My dear, you not only look more and more like your lovely mother, you show the benefit of her training, and her fine Maryland manners."

"Thank you!" But the compliment did not please her. Two cars drove in, both local, and from the direction of the warm-up ring came the sharp squeal of an angry horse, and the crack of a fenceboard being kicked. She excused herself, lodging her duties and responsibilities more firmly in her mind as she went, and averting her gaze from a row of trailers as penance for her hope; lots of times older exhibitors didn't even show up the first afternoon, which was mostly for Pony Club, anyway.

"I don't want green," said John. "I want white, and we took some to the last horse show. I saw them. Mother said you packed the tack trunk, so you must have lost them."

"I didn't lose them." Henry, mindful of his departure, found patience astonishingly easy. "Besides, Teddy would look stupid in exercise bandages."

"You don't know that. Anyway, they cost five dollars a set, and I'm going to tell mother you lost them."

"I didn't."

"Then find them."

"What do I care. I don't care about the stupid bandages."

"They were your responsibility."

"I don't see why you're so grouchy."

"I'm not grouchy." Talbot Light had arrived. He'd said, "John did you say your name was? You're fifteen?"

"Yes," John had replied. "I've stopped growing too," but Talbot Light had already looked away from him, toward Margaret, for Christ's sake. He had raised his voice and repeated himself: "We think that I stopped growing around Christmas."

"What?"

"I'm five eight and a half."

"What? Yes, of course. Tall family." That had been all. He had offered to stay out of their hair, to find a hotel in town and to pick up some breakfast on his own. "Nonsense," Kate had demurred, but the judge had insisted, and John had been unable to bring himself to the man's notice since. He braided and rebraided, soaped and resoaped, polished and repolished. Every square millimeter of his equipment gleamed, but there was no white, nothing to catch a judge's eye in a maelstrom of browns and blacks, subdued canaries and well-bred blues. The only white hairs on Teddy were his whiskers, and in the interest of perfection, those had to go. He turned to Henry. "You lost them, you find them."

"You don't need them."

"Just shut up, all right?"

Henry shrugged and strolled away.

The bandages were what he had settled on. That he knew they would look ridiculous made him the more angry that they couldn't be found. He could tell that Henry wouldn't find them, wouldn't even look, and that if he went to mother, she would say, "What do you want them for anyway? Surely not Teddy? Don't be silly," walking away from him, not even looking at him, thinking of something else besides his need, anything else, as ever. Teddy shifted his weight, nearly treading on John's toe. "You asshole," he said. "You big fucking asshole." Then he looked around, but mother was nowhere to be seen.

Peter appeared, saying, "Have you seen the wire cutters?" as if the wire cutters were significant.

"What for?"

"I don't know. They want them at the judge's stand for something."

"What did he say to you?"

"Who?"

"Talbot Light, who else?"

"I don't know. 'Do you have any wire cutters? We need some wire cutters here.' Something."

"Did he speak to you by name?"

"I guess so."

"Jesus!"

"Well, he knows my name."

"I think you should stay out of his hair."

"It wasn't . . ."

"It's hard enough to be impartial when the exhibitors aren't hanging on to you every minute."

"Hey, what's with you?"

"Nothing, but I think you should let me take him the wire cutters."

"You're crazy."

"Just let me."

"Go ahead, but you've got to find them first." He agreed so easily that John got angry, wanting to shout something about, well, maybe Peter didn't think he had to make Light notice him, maybe he thought he was that good, well, they would just see, they would just see. Peter wandered away. The set of his shoulders was so beautiful that John wanted to shoot him.

Night. A sharp slam. Door? Shutter? A table collapsing with its burden of costly equipment? Axel sat up in bed, instantly alert, and peered out the window. Nothing. He listened. Nothing more. He shrugged, but continued to gaze at the barns, the paddocks, the tent, the hotdog stand, the bright driveway and the dim trees. The air was thick with humidity, almost itself white, almost itself coverlets or clouds. It was both unpleasant and terribly reassuring to breathe.

Kate was asleep in her bed behind the wall. He could hear her characteristic aborted snore, more of a grumble than anything else. But she was everywhere too, except in his room, which seemed hooked on by the window to the real kingdom of farm life. He felt that if he gazed through it long enough, left it open wide enough, his room would spread out and thin, attach itself tight as lichen to the orb where she was ubiquitous.

Even thinking this he thought it was absurd. Could he really love this woman that he so frequently disapproved of? How had she not failed him? As his wife, she offered little in the way of warmth, or understanding, or even conversation. As the mother of his children she had shown impatience with their infancies, blindness to their individual talents and desires, inflexibility in her determination to propel one or more of them into the track of her own ambitions. As a sexual object, even the object of lust from afar, she was worn out. As an intellect, she was narrow and getting narrower. Yet the list of indictments (which he broke off voluntarily, knowing that he could go, and had gone, on and on) meant nothing. There, out the window, behind the wall, closed into every closet and tack trunk, folded in every blanket, entwined with dandy brushes, scrub brushes, hair brushes, toilet brushes, tooth brushes, was life itself. He felt that the more he

181

considered her, the more he was considering the mystery of life.

He tried to remember other women he had known. His mother, aunts, cousins, early girlfriends, the two women he'd flirted with since Kate's lightning conversion. Fine women, most of them. Generous, informative, motherly, passionate, but he had never felt in his encounters with them that he was encountering the world itself.

Love, as far as he could tell, had nothing to do with what one got or didn't get, even with reciprocity or gratitude, or kindness. Love, in fact, had nothing to do with individual histories. She was Kate and he, Axel, but his recent flirtation had nothing to do with his love for her, small, old, prejudiced, and petty persons that they were, and yet he loved her, he loved her, he loved her. His soul lived, in the end, to attach itself to the world she incorporated as easily as she drank her morning tea. Axel shook his head and laughed. Was any prey as virginal, as shy and wary of capture, as one's wife of twenty years?

Margaret, too, was wide-eyed. The noise had entered her dream as the sound of Peter falling off his horse, and the dream had wakened her.

By the clock it was four-thirty. In half an hour the alarm would ring, and she would commence with her chores, so that, instead of falling back to sleep, she sat up, and she too looked out the window, which faced away from the barns and the driveway, across the west field, where four horses could be discerned in the shadows of a copse of trees. Even as she watched, they drifted single file out of the woods across a moonlit rise of ground, heads heavy, tails swinging, bodies relaxed in the odd rocking gait of serene equines. Rosie, Stonewall, Count Down, Tiptop. Then she realized that these were the wrong names; these were names from four or five years ago. Rosie had been sold to someone in California, Stonewall had been killed in a hunting accident near Chicago, Count Down was on loan to a friend of mother's, and Tiptop . . . where was Tiptop? She couldn't remember. Nor could she remember the names of the current foursome. They had paused to graze, but now lifted their weighty heads and strolled toward the house. They passed from view again but their names didn't occur to her, although the names of countless others did: John Hancock, Downey's Gal, Dinky, Oscar, Jelly Bean, Jiminy Cricket. She could not remember which ones were still around, or how the others had come to depart, or even if they had owned and cared for all the names that flooded her. What, then, had she done in the past year that the minute knowledge of every animal on the farm, which was in a way the minute knowledge of her own history, had escaped her?

There were other things she couldn't remember now that she thought of them: her college roommate's real name, the names of most of her teachers, the face of the one freshman boy she had dated twice (though she could remember his yellow slacks and the way, when he sat down, he smoothed both palms down the insides of his thighs as if the fabric distressed him). What had they spoken of on those two dates? Why had he asked her out a second time? Surely she hadn't bored him with mother, the farm, Herbie, her brothers, for those six or eight hours they'd spent alone (alone?) together. When she thought of the yellow slacks, though, she was visited with the flavor of those months, the sensation of thinking so hard about one subject that thought itself was exhausting, and the subject, while still attractive, was also repellent, as if the brain recoiled from exerting itself any longer. Ah, then, yes. She had gone on and on about her home and her family. Not so much on the first date. On the first date she had made a conscientious effort, but on the second date she had talked and he had nodded and sipped his beers and taken her home at eleven-fifteen, and she had been too wound up in her obsession to feel ashamed.

Now, at home, she felt ashamed.

So what had become of her this summer? Nothing about the farm or the horses held her as they had at Bennett. The bolts that screwed her flat to this scene outside and all the other of all her days had broken. She couldn't remember these horses and she didn't care. She expected no longer to win her classes or to shine on Herbie, and she didn't care. She remembered a boy on a buckskin at some show, maybe this summer, who had been looking fixedly at his booted toe. Now it seemed to her that this was the story of her life; for as many years as she could remember, she had been staring at one booted toe or the other, understanding somehow that if she looked up and looked around, everything about the horses and the farm would become trivial. And now that she had thought these thoughts, what was she to do?

Four forty-five. What did people do, after all? More basically, how did they know what there was to do? Muffy (her roommate, what was her real name?) was intending to be a curator. How had she found out about that, how had it even occurred to her? Other girls had intended to be other things: an actuary, a kindergarten teacher, a housewife, an archeologist, a newspaper reporter. At the time, such occupations had been merely words to her, phrases whose meaning she had understood, but that meant nothing to her imagination. Mother was none of these things.

Once she'd intended to be a nun. After that her ambition was breeding horses. Now there was nothing. What did one do when all the obsessions drained away? Five o'clock. The alarm blared a moment before she punched it, and for the first time in her willing life, what she was getting up to accomplish seemed like work.

"Well, you can't ride your bicycle today, and that's final. How can you be so ridiculous? I need your help."

"Mrs. Karlson." Ellen Eisen held up the broken cheek strap of Spanky's bridle, managing at one and the same time to distract Kate's wrath from Henry ("Yes, dear?" she said in the affectionate tones she used with her favorite paying students) and to prove her major contention, that her time was precious and Henry owed it to her to stay around acting helpful.

"Henry," she said, and he turned immediately, dropping his bicycle on the grass and running for the hand riveter. She had not, at least, asked to inspect the old black saddle bag behind the seat of his vehicle, where he'd stored three peanut butter sandwiches, the remains of a box of raisins, a can of salted nuts, six sugar cookies, two cans of soda, his rain poncho, and a somewhat rusted pocketknife he'd found three weeks ago in one of the tack trunks. She had not frisked him, thereby discovering the folded one-dollar bills and handfuls of coins that comprised his travel fund, and the fact that he was wearing three layers of clothes (two shirts, a pair of shorts, clean pajamas, and a pair of slacks, as well as his largest shoes with two pairs of socks). Nor had she looked narrowly into his eyes and espied the imminence of his escape, as he'd feared she could. When he ran off to get the leather-working tool, therefore, he was elated rather than let down. The initial escape, perhaps the real escape, had been made. Pedaling away would now be a somewhat routine formality.

And besides, her strictures on the bicycle decided him about the family class. Departure, henceforth a foregone conclusion, could be put off another day. After delivering the riveter, he went to the hotdog stand, where the vendor, only just setting up but understanding Henry with perfect wordlessness, took out a moment and made him a celebratory hotdog. Mustard, catsup, relish, and kraut.

He felt himself a monolith of detachment. He had never been quite this happy before. Judging by his parents and siblings, as well as the rest of the post-twelve-year-old world, he might never be so again. Food, clothes, money, wheels, raincoat: in the event of a disaster, he could easily float away to higher ground.

"Hey, come here!" called John as Henry passed the barn door. "Go get me a cloth for my boots." He stood just inside Teddy's stall, looking traditionally resplendent: black hat, white stock, gold pin, black coat, buff breeches, liquid black boots. This was all wool stuff; their usual summer horse-show attire was more informal.

"Gosh!" muttered Henry.

John blushed. "Just get the cloth, would you? There's one on the hay bale out there somewhere."

Henry handed it to him, and he led Teddy from the stall. The bandages had been found, And, apparently, washed. White beribboned braids, bleached saddle pad. Tail like cornsilk, hooves painted, whiskers and ears neatly trimmed. "He looks like the town fruit," said Henry.

"Oh, shut up. Now listen. When I get on, I want you to take that cloth and rub the toes of my boots and the back parts, wherever you see any dust. Got it?" He settled himself into the sunlit, burnished saddle. "That's right. Now fold it up and run it over his head and neck and under his stomach. Stand up, you idiot." He gave Teddy a jerk in the mouth. Henry did as he was told. "Wipe off his hocks." Even these, usually stained no matter how hard you scrubbed, even these shone. Henry polished them and smoothed a few hairs of the tail. John was arranging himself, patting his breeches, puffing his stock. "O.K. I'm going to warm up. Go get me a hotdog and meet me back here in fifteen minutes."

"Where's your thirty-five cents?" But John was already trotting away. Because, somehow, his brother did look vaguely ridiculous, too formal, overwarm, already sweating, Henry fished the quarter and the dime out of his brass-hard back pocket and headed for the hotdog stand. Upon buying a soda as

186

well ("They're not cold yet, young man," said some strange and officious mother), he went back to the spot and rewarded himself for his generosity with only one small bite.

John returned even more red-faced, having been greeted with good-natured whistles and hoots. He snatched the hotdog from Henry, griping about the missing bite, then dripped mustard on his breeches. ("Shit," he said, then, "Give me some of that, too," reaching for the Coke.) In the interval since mounting, he had donned lovely pale yellow riding gloves, trimmed in narrow brown, set with holes in patterns like jewels. Henry had never seen anything like them around the farm before. Mother treated their string gloves with jealous anxiety: doling them out and calling them in, practically putting them on their very hands and snatching them off. "How'd you pay for those?" he asked.

"None of your business. I charged them, actually." They both smiled. This was indeed a victory. Awed, Henry pursued the matter no further. "Here," said John, handing over his litter. "It's almost time for my class." He turned Teddy to go, then paused. "Hey," he said, "why are you wearing your pajamas under your pants?" Henry looked down. The cowboy-patterned legs, which he had so carefully folded up to his knees, had dropped down over his shoes. He shrugged. John shrugged. "Wish me luck," said the older boy.

"Good luck," said Henry, wanting to say more.

And here he was. Kate, although she knew better, couldn't repress an appreciative "hmm!" as Peter trotted into the ring, and even then she would have admitted that the judge's sudden alertness was not unintended by her, lifelong good sport though she considered herself. The horse, MacDougal, and the rider, her own son Peter, did look extraordinary. Light put down his glass of ice water and leaned forward. The course was a large and complex one, designed not by Kate but by a local horseman who had brought over a few of his own jumps. It was basically a four-legged serpentine with a fifth leg that crossed the others at a sharp angle. Without knowledge of the line, the arrangement of jumps looked chaotic, and a number of them could not be taken straight on. It began and ended with wide brush fences, four feet nine and four feet eleven respectively. The other fences were somewhat smaller, but quite as intimidating.

Peter's warm-up circle was exquisitely round, and seemed to be generated by vigilance itself. MacDougal tossed his head, his ears flicking backward. But the anger was momentary. With some weight or finger signal that Kate couldn't see, Peter soothed the horse and moved him into an alert canter. In his practiced and stylish way, MacDougal gathered himself for the fence, shortening his own last stride, pricking his ears until the tips almost touched, bringing his back hooves and hocks deep under himself, then taking off. Peter rocked forward in perfect harmony, so perfect that Kate could feel it in her own body and had to stifle an utterance. The horse jumped big, nonchalantly, tucking his black hooves against his elbows for a split second, then he galloped on. Three strides and he was ready for the rails, then they made the first 180-degree turn, and were already over the chicken coop that stood just a stride out of it. "Watch his head," Kate wanted to say to the judge, "watch my son's head." It turned with the readiest calmness, computing the line, tallying the jumps, seeming of itself to guide and rate the horse; seeming of itself to predict, a moment later, the exact same turning of the horse's head. Gallop, gather, leap, gallop, gather, leap. It was hypnotic. Talbot Light made no sound or movement until the last, huge fence, when, as the horse sprang, the judge stood a little out of his seat. Clean round, no time faults. In open jumping classes, winning was mathematical: the other two horses in the jump-off were big leapers, but not smooth. Either of them could do it. Kate bit her lip.

As the jump crew ran in and raised the fences three inches, it was clear to Kate that Peter should make no mistakes. Style had impressed Talbot so far, but the impression could only be nailed into place with successful tactics and visible tact. The jump crew scattered to the rails, and the announcer called out Peter's number. Go slow, Kate thought. The key to a good time was corner cutting, not rushing. He entered as quietly as before, as if the course before him were a three-foot practice course, twice around. As quietly, he settled deep into the saddle; as quietly, he faced the obstacles one by one; as quietly, he shaved his corners until Kate wanted to close her eyes; as quietly, he kept the horse in perfect balance from the first stride to the last. Now it was Light's turn to grunt involuntarily. This, perhaps, was the highest compliment, because it showed that this jaded judge's soul was actually moved. He said nothing, however, and did not look at Kate. Each of the other two horses knocked down a pole.

When Peter brought Mac in to accept the blue, the horse shied at the photographer. "Never without something up his sleeve, that animal," she said gaily. "Smile for goodness' sake, don't you like to win?" Peter stood up straight, acted as if he liked to win, and smiled, not for the camera, but for his mother. "I love you," she said. It seemed perfectly natural at the time.

"Your brothers are doing very well today."

The voice, instantly familiar, shocked Margaret, so that she pretended to find a hair in her tunafish sandwich and to remove it very carefully. She looked up. Harrison Randolph looked more adult than ever. "Yes, they are. Better than I am by a long shot." Peter had won both his jumping classes. John had taken the open working hunter, as well as second in his equitation class.

"Are you disappointed?" He smiled.

"No, not really." She thought of confessing her nighttime revelation of indifference but did not, both because it seemed disloyal to the farm to admit it now, when there were so many

189

strangers peering about, and because one confession could lead to another and another. She moved over and he sat down, miraculously. He had come. He looked very handsome, and she feared that he would allude to her failure to get in touch with him. Oh, indeed, he looked very, very handsome.

He said, "Winning gets less important, maybe." She was relieved. "When you're grown up."

She blushed. "Well, I . . ."

"You are grown up, aren't you? I thought I heard you say something about that once." His eyes were bright with mockery.

"I haven't seen your gray."

"I'm saving him for the combined event."

"He's sound, then."

"Of course. I'm not cruel, you know." He was still laughing. "Really I'm not."

Again she noticed how he said the words "I" and "you" in the oddest way, as if they contained a freightload of significance. Undoubtedly a simple trick of speech, perhaps even a regionalism, yet each time he said either he aroused both her interest and her resentment. She wished to look at him, but also to go away. "I believe you," she said.

"Look at me."

She did so.

"You're very pretty." He smiled that smile of Peter's and she thought, yes, she was very pretty. It would be good to remember that. He added, "It's a good thing you didn't call me that night." Margaret coughed, and when he did not elaborate, began, "My moth . . ."

"Yes, I did see your mother drive past with those people from Chicago, the Smelt somethings."

"The Meltzers."

"Yes, it's a good thing." Now his eye was upon her.

"Why?" She tried for a flat, cool tone, and attained something between a squeak and a bark.

"Look at me." He put the tip of his finger beneath her chin. "I did have designs."

It was hard to keep looking at him, but she made herself. His eyes were not brown but dark hazel. Their color made him seem less sinister, in spite of his "designs." He was not so handsome after all, and he was old, like someone's uncle. It was uncles who always told you you were very pretty, and while predicting unprecedented social success for you, stepped aside, out of the running. "So you say," she replied.

"Mmmm." In a moment he said, "My wife is coming back from the Orient next week. She's been gone nearly five months."

"Does she work there?" Margaret skated over the "she" as delicately as possible.

"She studies. She's a jade specialist at the Smithsonian."

Their previous chatter fell away, and Margaret sat up attentively. "How did she get to be that?"

"Well, she went to Stanford. . . ."

"I mean, how did she get the idea?"

"Her father was a famous Sinologist, and they lived in Taiwan for a good deal of her childhood. She was born in China."

"Oh."

"You sound disappointed."

"I am. She didn't just think of it. I keep wondering how people just think of things to do. Do you have a real job?"

"You could call it that. I'm a stockbroker, but it's hardly something I thought of. I work for my uncle."

"Hnnh."

"My uncle would be insulted at your tone. He has lots of theories on the philosophical profundities of the stock market. But, yes, you may sneer. Anyway, some people do just think of things. My sister is a primatologist, and there hasn't been a primate in our family for years." He chuckled, but Margaret did not respond. "She got the idea at college, I think."

"Yeah?" She tried to sound polite, but there was no hope, in spite of the primatologist. Surprisingly, as she looked toward the warm-up ring where her brother was mounting Teddy, across the driveway and past the house and barn that formed the arena of her memory, tears started down her cheeks. "Good Lord," said Harrison Randolph.

"I'm sorry." She snorted and wiped her eyes on her sleeve. This bout, she could tell, was going to be a plentiful one. "I don't know anything to do. I don't even know how to find out." She snorted again. And would every man always bring out the most moist, least attractive facets of her being? He offered her his handkerchief.

"You know why I went into selling stocks? It seemed very innocuous. Nothing wrong with making money, right? Are you O.K.? Look." He raised his voice slightly. "None of my friends knew what they wanted to do until they were about thirty. By then, of course, there was the wife and the house and the kids, or maybe the dissertation, and anyway they'd been doing what they now didn't want to do for eight or ten years."

Margaret gave a huge, shuddering sigh. Harrison leaned forward and pulled off his boots one by one. Then he wiggled his toes and made a face. Still she would not smile. "There's another thing, too. When you're younger you love lots of things. Baseball cards, model trains. You wouldn't believe the model train my father built me, with all sorts of tunnels and levels, even a waterfall that the train ran under without getting wet. My sister used to wring her hands and run out of the room every time I switched it through there because she thought I was going to be electrocuted. Ah, what a train! After that came the horses, and I was terribly avid, almost possessed. I thought I'd never get to the bottom of that one. Then it was girls. Women, I mean. Sorry." He glanced at Margaret's sober countenance, and said, "Are you afraid you won't find something that goes as deep as the horses do, or did?"

Margaret nodded and put her hands over her face.

"Don't fall for the two temptations."

"What are those?" Her voice was barely audible.

"Marriage and trying to do over and over what you did before. Marriage doesn't work the way you think it's going to." He cleared his throat. "And doing the same thing over and over again is incredibly boring. Even riding. Why do you think masters of hounds always fall asleep in their chairs right after dinner?"

Margaret wiped his handkerchief, which was enormous, over her cheeks and chin.

"My sister stays out in the jungle in Venezuela for years on end. When she comes home she turns her nose up at the accoutrements of civilization and pines away for monkeys. I envy her, even though she isn't very nice and doesn't have any friends, only colleagues, and the jungle and its various diseases have really taken their toll of her looks. I don't know. Do you feel better? All your choices are before you, my dear."

The handkerchief was now soaked, as were both sleeves of her shirt, but the tears had abated. She sniffed a couple of times, and was able to look at him again. "I don't have any choices."

"Yes, well, sit with me for a minute or so." He smiled very sweetly, designs or no.

The afternoon cooled with the approach of dinnertime and the rising of a breeze that was almost springlike in its fragrance. There were five families in the ring, one of them, the Wards from Kansas City, consisting of eight members. Hillyard Ward, eighteen months, slumped against his father's arm, but the rest of the family sat up chipper and straight, expecting to win.

Axel, Kate, Peter, John, Henry, and Margaret were ranged next to them, mounted on six of Kate's flashy home-bred bays. They were a striking group, two blond, four dark,

193

three rangy, three compact, all six perfectly accoutered, all six attesting, for the time being, to the wisdom of Kate's theories and methods. Even Axel's legs hung limber but still at just the proper angle. All their hands and wrists were set in the mold of Kate's hands and wrists (although during more strenuous activities the results of Kate's old accident were apparent in the way she held her arm rather high), all their backs were supple and firm, like hers, and more upright, perhaps, than the Wards' backs or the Jordans' backs on the other side of them, because Kate's theories were more German than Bob Ward's or Ella Jordan's. A few of the Pony Club mothers, who were yearly fascinated by this display of Karlsons, knew nothing about theories, but they remarked how proud and somewhat reserved the family looked, how their family solidarity as well as their equestrian ease was epitomized by that slightly exaggerated upright posture. Once a year, a few of the mothers took time out to envy Kate, whose family, in contrast to theirs, was centripetal rather than centrifugal. Not one riding child, one hospital volunteer, one football player, all of whom had to be driven everywhere all the time, but four intelligent children who stayed at home and knew one another, day in, day out. Everybody at the dinner table, and no rule about it to be enforced.

Herbert Eisen paused in his winding up of extension cords and admired the Karlsons, too. Behind them as they sat there expertly controlling their horses, around them as they trotted down one side of the ring, were their own trees, their own fences, their own rolling fields, as far as the eye could see. The place was, even this late in the summer, so green, so breezy, so refreshing: streams, ponds, fruit trees, horses, cats, geese, pastoral order on every hand. And such a handsome family, he had to admit. Peter, of course, was the beauty and Margaret actually rather plain, but on the whole Eisen found it pleasant to look at the Karlsons. No one fat, everyone, even Axel (whom Eisen knew for a fact to be a real workaholic), sun-browned and obviously active. Each of the children was quite well mannered, and their mother never seemed to show the usual middle-aged strains of fatigue and harassment.

Eisen heard two mothers murmuring behind him about how their children spent more time here than they did in their own homes, and he smiled. Ellen, too, but who could blame them? The mothers, and perhaps he, himself, would have done the same had they been children. He knotted the last of the cords, then began to pour out tubs of melted ice. He felt, not exactly envious, but not exactly serene, either. He snapped at one little boy, but also smiled at the two mothers, and one of them said of Kate, "She's really something, isn't she?" Eisen nodded.

The Wards did win. The judge handed the blue ribbon to Hillyard, who promptly put it in his mouth, and the trophy to Mrs. Ward, who smiled and mentioned that next year there would be another tiny entrant in the family class, if everything went well. The ringmaster repeated this over the microphone, and the audience applauded again. The Karlsons were the last out of the ring. For a moment, alone center stage, it was apparent that everything was indeed theirs, intruding Wards notwithstanding. The ringmaster thanked them for their hospitality, and the applause for them was even louder than for the others. Here, the ringmaster seemed to be saying, was success of a very particular and rare nature. Kate smiled her glorious smile, Axel shaded his eyes, and Herbert Eisen thought to himself that who, at this moment, did not want to be them?

❧10❧

IN the morning Henry was there one minute ("Peanut butter for breakfast," said John. "Yuk!") and gone the next. The legs of his pajamas were pinned with safety pins, and included in the black saddle bag were two pairs of underpants, forgotten the day before. He was less enthusiastic about going than he was filled with conviction. It was this conviction that carried him nonchalantly past mother, coming out of the main barn (he'd thought she was still in the house) and without a wobble past father, who, hammer in hand, was walking the fence line looking for loose boards. He looked up as Henry passed, and Henry waved. Axel shouted, "Be back before lunch," and then there was the sharp sudden sound of his hammer on wood. That, thought Henry, is that, and it was almost difficult, although inevitable, to keep pedaling. He swayed himself around the S curve, past the four

Thoroughbreds who were grazing near the fence, past the red-winged blackbird, who rose out of her nest, as usual, and made a feint for his head. He pedaled faster, steering hard into the left-hand rut. He made himself think of the miles of exfoliating asphalt ahead of him, and dropped over the lip of the hill, holding tight and staring toward the first appearance of the bridge. With luck, no cars. No cars. As he shot through, he shouted, "Goodbye! Goodbye! Goodbye!," which lifted his spirits slightly, and then he began the long struggle up the far hill.

It was almost difficult enough, after all, to encourage him to turn back, but still the journey had little to do with his wishes, everything to do with his fate. He pumped and pumped. Here were father's stalls, here the gates. A car approached and he stopped, pretending no interest in the road outside the gates. Two Pony Clubbers waved. He waved back. The car crept down the hill behind him, and soon the coast was clear. Left foot to left pedal. He readjusted his saddle bag, his clothing. He coughed. He checked the brake, although it had always worked. Now then. Here was his silver, here were his greenbacks. He thought of meat, potatoes, fruit, vegetables. At last he jumped down on the higher, left pedal and was, although still visible for at least the next five minutes, gone.

This was what they would say about him: "He's done wonders with that horse, really. One of Kate's most impossible mounts, you know. Comparisons are odious, but he's almost as good, if not . . . Well, for his age . . . and there's nearly two years' difference." "Excellent equestrian." "Why not Team material? I really think . . ." The imagined dialogues made his stomach churn, made him perspire. It was not comfortable, really, to think about them, but as he worked around Teddy, forking up manure, then laying new bedding, he could hardly help himself. The worst, he knew, was that he half believed them. When pairs of spectators or other riders that he knew went by, he found himself trying to catch words, then he found himself, yes, disappointed that they were talking of their own concerns.

Besides, the dressage scores weren't even posted yet. His had compared favorably with Peter's, but the division was large. Any idiot really could simply appear. Any two or three idiots. He and Peter weren't charmed by any means. Or were they? Teddy grunted and sank his snout deep into the water bucket. A moment later he dripped a long thread of water and saliva across the front of John's shirt, but John paid only cursory attention. He was thinking, "Amazing how those two are always so closely matched, more than brothers, really almost as if they were . . ."

The hypothetical twin appeared in the doorway. "Mrs. Jensen from Omaha took it, but not by much. I was second, you were third."

"She's not going to get that mare over the water to save her life. Who was fourth?"

"Some new guy. Mother's never seen the horse, either. That sort of Morgany-looking brown with the white spots on his chest."

"I didn't think he was so good."

Peter shrugged. It was remarkable how neat he looked, same breeches, same boots, same tie, no stains or even wrinkles. John had had to go back to his summer clothes, so spotted and rumpled was his formal winter costume. He turned away. The subject of his brother was suddenly too complex and too compelling to admit of new matter. How had he managed, for fifteen years, simply to get along? To talk with this enigma, to work with him, but especially to fight with him? For a long time, before father had converted the upstairs porch, they had shared a room. There had been fights over space, over cleaning up, over mislaid and broken possessions. To think that there was a person he himself had been who was able to yell at and even punch Peter. He wanted to ask, "Am I as weird to you as you are

198

to me?" but he couldn't, and besides, the inevitable reply would be "I don't know," Peter's most characteristic utterance, perhaps the linchpin of his mysteriousness. Peter's mysteriousness. How laughable that idea would have been six months before. "Go away," said John. "I've got secret stuff to do."

"I'll bet. Like cleaning his feet again; he's standing right in it."

The gray mare went over the water jump after two refusals, and the Morgany brown balked at, of all things, a little picket fence. Teddy galloped around the cross-country at terrific speed, and seemed rather surprised at the end, throwing his head around and flicking his ears as if his plans had gone awry. There were jumps John knew Teddy had wanted to pause for and think about, but there had been no time to pause. John whipped and Teddy galloped headfirst over everything. Their time was jolting: forty-five seconds faster than Peter's and well ahead of everyone else. He dismounted to a few raised eyebrows and remarks by Lambert Smith about discretion being the better part of sportsmanship, but he interpreted their disapproval as perverse praise. What a time! How could they not be impressed?

"I think he's actually a bit more daring, bolder, you might say, than the older one," went the dialogue in his mind, "perhaps even better material for an international career. I won't say anything about style, there is two years' difference, after all. . . ." Best to be careful about the legs, he thought, recalling mother's saying, "Wreckless riders ruin tendons," but Teddy was in excellent condition and a little blowout had probably done him a world of good. Still, he got out the liniment and slapped it on, all the way up and all the way down. They walked and walked. Teddy, for the moment, was almost too tired to eat, but it would be hours till the arena jumping.

Here came Peter. John dropped his eyes modestly, and pretended to be peering into Teddy's ears. There were no congratulations, however, not even any sound except the crunch of Peter's boots on the gravel, approaching, retreating. Always in a daze, the boy! But when John looked up, Peter's glance, just turning away, caught his for the briefest second. Still no word, not even the most minimally polite, not the least word of a stranger unfamiliar with the struggles and disappointments of the summer. "Hey!" said John, but Peter walked away. When he was very far away, John screamed, "I beat you! I beat you and you can't even admit it! Some good sport you are, your mother's son if you ask me! Hey! *Hey!*" but Peter didn't turn around, didn't pause, didn't even repeat the trivial eye contact he had made before. "Come on!" said John to Teddy, who had dropped his nose to snuffle the gravel drive, and they marched in a small circle, cooling out.

Kate said, "I've never seen anything so ridiculous and infuriating." He should not have expected praise. He kept his head down and worked assiduously around Teddy in his stall, picking up minuscule traces of manure and single wet straws. "Why do you persist in this perversity? Why do you want to lame or kill one of my horses, and break your own neck to boot? That would be a great inconvenience, let me tell you! You could not have gotten poor Teddy around the course in that kind of time without beating him unmercifully from start to finish!" John's head popped up, his mouth open. "Don't speak to me! I don't want to hear it, do you understand? I expect, after thirteen years on horseback, that you will show some kind of judgment, that you will show that you know more than these bloody hamhanded farmboys who learn how to win ribbons and wreck good horseflesh all in the space of a year! I've got principles! A hard enough thing to hold on to in this business without someone like you, someone of my own flesh and my own raising . . ." Her voice cracked, then she paused, and went on more quietly. "Listen to me! All over this country horses are a big business. Racing, horseshowing, foxhunting, all of it. And everybody, *everybody* except the fortunate wealthy few, has to do it on a shoestring. Do you know what I've seen? Don't speak. Now it's your turn to listen for once. I've seen Tennessee Walkers leaning, *leaning* against *walls* because they were blistered under their boots and couldn't stand up. These same animals a half an hour later in the show ring are lifting their poor feet as high as they can and rolling their eyes at the whip. I've seen jumpers forced to pick up their legs over a fence by trainers who whap them with nailed jump poles and naked electric wires. People stud the inside surfaces of training reins with sharp tacks because they're too impatient to teach their cattle horses to neck rein the right way. All over this country there are three- and four-year-old Thoroughbreds that are broken down already from running too often on racetracks that are too hard, five-year-olds with all the nerves in their legs cut so they can't feel the pain when they run. Babies! *Babies!* I can't bear it! Listen to *me! I can't bear it and I've taught you differently!* Don't you dare speak to me. Am I to sit by and watch the growth of cruelty in my own son? Going too fast, faster than you know you should, than you know your horse is capable of, is just as bad as all that. Yes, you're shocked! I'm still shocked when I think of all the blood, the blood of horses, shed in the attempt just to win. We don't do that here, and if you must do it by some horrible inner compulsion, then you can just leave and welcome."

"I . . ."

"No. I don't want any apologies. If that horse is sound by my standards, you may participate in the arena jumping. If I ever see you or hear of you doing what you did today, or anything like it, I will pull you off my horses forever, got that? Oh, my God. Oh, *God!*"

It was frightening. She seemed to John red and constricted, as if only a larger body could contain her anger. He looked at her in utter silence, afraid that something awful would happen, more awful than a simple blow aimed at him, more awful than continued fury, something like death, perhaps. He expected her to tell him at last that she hated him and always had, but she did not. She merely said, "Oh, God," again in a much more subdued tone, then, "Bring the horse to me when you're saddled up." She turned carefully and walked carefully away. Once she coughed. He would have said it, he thought, if he hadn't been such a coward. He would have said that for now and always he hated her to the very center of his being, to the very center of hers.

When Kate was ashamed of herself, she grew all the more cheerful, had all the more words of encouragement and blessing to bestow on the lesson girls, the Pony Club mothers and fathers. She grew smiling and radiant in direct proportion to her shame, and nothing shamed her, ultimately, more than rage. Already the thought niggled at her that she had said too much, made her point too emphatically. Of course she was right, but when she walked out of the stable she was already beaming, eager to resolve any problems that might have arisen in the last five minutes or so. Only Axel was lingering nearby. She smiled at him, and, in spite of the yelling he had no doubt just heard, he smiled back. He had gotten handsomer of late. Perhaps it was his summer tan, perhaps he had taken off a few pounds. Surely he hadn't always been this thin, this lithe, this alluringly bow-legged. Well, yes, he had been bow-legged—she had a dim memory of liking that about him in the beginning, when she would sometimes hang back on busy streets so that she could watch him walk so bow-leggedly and energetically through the crowds. She smiled more brightly and paused, sensing for a moment the feel of those first months in New York, dressed in woolens and high heels, always in a hurry, but a glad hurry. He'd had two job offers that fall, one in New York and one that had led to the position he now held, to the establishment of the farm, to, in short, everything now irrevocable and fixed in their lives. As she paused, she wanted to ask him if he regretted, not the life, but the job itself, the piece of work that he had done compared to the piece of work that he might have done had she not wanted so desperately to get out into the countryside. She glanced around herself. This they could not have had in Connecticut, not on any realistically imaginable salary.

It was not that he wouldn't have answered her. Perhaps, both honestly and tactfully, he would have said that the work was better, the job suited him, the street-level office was more human than a skyscraper cubicle would have been, that he was glad to have molded his work to his own desires (she assumed he had done so—he would have mentioned it if he had not, wouldn't he?). There would not have been time, in the city, for life (for reading projects and land negotiations and . . . whatever else he did). Surely he would agree. No, it was not fear of his response that made her reach out and touch him, very quickly, as she paused, but then stride on. It was the simple impossibility of asking such a question, of breaking so far out of their common habits. Still, she knew that she had smiled and touched him, and perhaps someday there would be a conversation, an easygoing recapitulation of a number of things, and in the course of it she could say, "Remember when they wanted to hire you . . ." and he would remember and all would be well for the rest of their lives.

With assiduous last-minute study, John got the course into his head. There didn't seem to be room for much else. When people spoke to him, he forgot to answer, and he kept finding strap ends he had left out of their keepers, and bits of dirt and dust that he had failed to wipe off Teddy or himself. The more he resolved to remain unmoved by mother's tirade, the more confused and preoccupied he became. Here was Teddy eating again, for example, foaming his bit green, having his way after all these weeks.

The course, however, was the most important thing. It was complicated, with a number of tight turns and a couple of imposing jumps, including a final triple in-and-out over chicken coops that was a bit tricky because it was into the sun and four and a half strides after the previous fence, rather than four or five. The woman on the gray mare, who'd walked beside him as they inspected the obstacles, had muttered, "Diabolical," after they'd paced it out, and John thought of her mare's long, spindly legs and high center of gravity. "Best to be sure of your lead here," he'd said heartily, but she didn't answer. Peter was well ahead of them, walking alone, his head down, his calculations and reactions, as always, unknowable. Then John mounted and warmed up.

That he was second by only a few points meant less to him now than it had. In spite of his hatred of her, Kate's sneer at the word "winning" rather cowed him. He was ready, for the moment, to be a little more philosophical about the whole thing, to let the fates take their course. Knowing what to do and doing it were the important things, although obviously he wasn't going to hold back.

And it wasn't that he defied her, although from her position next to the rail she thought he did. He'd intended a deliberate negotiation of the fences, even a little bit slow, and he'd assumed, after their hard cross-country run, that Teddy would like nothing better. He carried his whip and wore his spurs more out of habit than anything else; they might come in handy with Teddy's career of stubbornness, and John knew he could control them. When his number was called, it was all set in his mind just how doggedly it would go, and exactly how many points he would lose to Peter, and he didn't really mind. But when he asked Teddy to canter, and turned him in the preliminary circle, he realized that the whip and the spurs were hardly necessary, not necessary at all. He did not intend to go fast, but habit and the tension in his body (there was mother, disapproving on the sidelines) took over. The circle was lumpy. The first fence loomed, and even Teddy seemed a little surprised, a little precipitate. John grew anxious. Inevitably, his hand tensed on the whip, and they went just that much faster.

After dropping his bicycle on the grass by the house, and making a tour of the refreshment stands (disappointing, but then it was very late, and the last day of the show), Henry sauntered near the rail with his gleanings: a warm cream soda, a Baby Ruth bar, two melting ice cubes wrapped in a napkin, and a package of Sweetarts. He was very hot. The cream soda cloyed in his throat, and the candy offered no relief. He was peeling bits of paper from the ice cubes when John came into the ring. John coming into the ring he had seen countless times, so he paid almost no attention. His tongue, his lips, his throat, yearned for the ice. It melted in his hand as he worked at the paper, leaving white streaks in the grime. At last. It was cool. It was cold. It hurt his hard palate, stung and froze his tongue, but his hands were awfully dirty. He spit it onto the back of his wrist, blew in and out of his aching mouth, took it again, spit it out again. This time, slippery, it got away and raised a little puff as it landed in the dust.

On the second turn of the course, a ninety-degree angle three strides before a nice-sized brush fence, Teddy slipped, then caught himself. There was a rustle among the spectators, a general intake of breath. Henry looked up. Teddy made the fence, though his arc was flat and effortful. John, unwontedly, was sitting very far forward, his legs tightly into the horse's sides, his hands way up on the horse's neck. Mother, Henry thought, would tease him about riding like an Italian.

He was very thirsty. He could see the people in charge beginning to dump the tubs of melted and melting ice on the ground and he wanted to shout or run over to them. There were only two left. His throat felt stuck together from the hot day and the soft drinks he had guzzled. John, he thought, ought to slow down. Here was the triple-in-and-out next, and the sun glaring right on it. They were pouring out the first of the two tubs. "Hey!" he shouted, surprising even himself, looking at once and automatically toward mother, across the ring, who warned them repeatedly about making noise when someone was on course. But his sound was lost in another sound: the sharp rap of hooves on wood, the sharp soprano gasp of lots of people. He turned his head to see Teddy's tail rising and rising, his shoulders, carried by momentum over, down, and finally, with a crack of wood, into the next part of the in-and-out, his head turning, instinctively, out of the way. And there was John himself arcing, John himself flipping over, John himself landing on the ridge of the third coop, the one with the target painted on it. Henry closed his eyes very tightly, and did not open them again until his brother was lost in a melee of first-aid people and Pony Club mothers.

Everyone thought she would welcome leftovers, and so there were hams and green bean casseroles and bowls of potato salad, a horrifying turkey, sliced and fitted back together, loaves of bread, and substances steeped in tomato paste and crusted with cheese. Even as Kate beamed upon, thanked, and blessed those who told her that only the good die young and that they had always noted John's special fey quality, she wanted to scream and smash their dreadful flowered dishes. There were so many of these people, and their sympathetic looks, like a swarm of little hands, light but thick, touching even her face, pinned her when she wanted to rise to the occasion.

The family, still appareled in hot sobriety, drifted around the food, then drifted away. All these priests and mothers bestowed long kindly glances upon them, as well, and Kate wanted to snatch her children out of range, as if they might be contaminated. She wanted even more, however, to be rid of the consolers, to go outside, and to resume, this day, this afternoon (a Wednesday, a perfectly good Wednesday), her ruptured routine. She had always hated these sorts of rituals—the last day of school, Thanksgiving, Christmas, and Easter. It was best to be in the midst of a great rhythm of days! How she longed to go outside and set up her chair on the Irish Bank, to call out the measured and thoughtful commands, to save herself with work. Here was the continuation of life: work. "Yes," she said, "thank you, God bless you, you're so kind." Across the room, Axel was doing the same thing: accepting what they put in his hands, nodding, looking suitably forlorn. It was sickening and she turned away.

Afterward, when she said, "Everyone in the saddle. Let's give a few of these animals a little exercise, anyway," Margaret and Henry refused, and Axel fixed her with a strange, long look that shamed her, so she said, heartily, "Fools to mope," knowing she sounded wrong and unmotherly.

"Mope?" said Axel.

"Well . . ." Kate smiled slightly, nakedly.

"Mope?"

Her black dress was wool, binding at the neckline and arm-holes, pricking her at the waist. She fingered the narrow belt. She would undress and put on clean shorts, then walk out to the broodmare pasture. Axel stepped close to her and put his hand lightly on hers, stilling the fingers. "Mope?" he said again.

"For God's sake, Axel!" Grief of the sort everyone expected had always been beyond her. She was terrific at nursing, arranging, caring for, galvanizing, steadying, breaking the news, but bad at this. "It was an accident!"

"Accident?"

"Well, of course!"

"Accident?"

Kate's mouth opened slightly and she blinked, wanting sud-denly to say, Axel? Axel? as if he were unconscious, or some awful nineteenth-century thing had happened to his reason, but when he said "Accident?" again, she realized that she had mistaken skepticism for confusion.

"Who did it?" she flared up. "You didn't do it! The horse didn't do it! I didn't do it! It happened! That's all, it happened!"

Peter appeared, dressed impeccably, a bit more formally than usual, and he said, "Nothing's had a bit of work since Sunday."

When she had changed her dress and met him at the stable, he did not mount, but walked beside her out to the training field, MacDougal's reins over his arm, the horse sniffing and blowing companionably behind. She found her chair and set it in the usual spot, but did not sit down. He mounted, and when he drew up to lengthen his stirrups, she adjusted the one on her side, then held it for his foot, and though she did it idly, as if not doing it at all, he knew it was unaccustomed behavior and appreciated its significance. She said, "I want you to pay close attention to his walk today. Try and sense the freedom of a free walk, the tightness of a collected walk. I want you to feel not that he's slowing down or speeding up, but that he's drawing his spine together or stretching it out. It may bore you, but let's spend most of the lesson time on the walk, O.K.?" When had she cared about boring him before?

He said, good student, "You always think jumping is going to be the hardest, but it's the simplest once you get going."

"Yes."

"One, two, three, four," she continued in a moment. "The walk is utterly foursquare, utterly deliberate, utterly straightforward." One. Two. Three. Four. Plop, plop, plop, plop. She loved the delicious and never sudden fall of hooves in the dust, the fluid alternation of movement in haunches, in shoulders, in the gay bobbing of MacDougal's head. The sound and the movement called forth the knowledge she had spent almost forty years accumulating, knowledge of bones and tendons and muscles and skin, of tact and strategy, of rules and the exceptions to rules. She closed her eyes. One, two, three, four, and the creak of leather and the jangle of hardware, and the fragrance of a breath of wind, just for a moment, all of these repeated things soothing her, calling from her her own repeated instructions. "Oh, dear," she thought, as she opened her eyes and her spirits rose. John, of course. But her spirits rose. She had not cried since the accident ("Accident?" said Axel) and now she was almost happy. "Collect him now, just a little!" and then, "Let him go!" One, two, three, four, she was lulled, and let herself believe that all things are repeated, that nothing is lost, that no one is at fault.

John. Of course. Her son, bone of her bone, the child in the womb (the first movements had always felt like air bubbles popping, then there had been the swimming from place to place, then the elbows and feet that had reassured her of their completeness). Since the accident where had been her motherly tears? Where her tender reminiscences? He still angered her, and now her spirits were rising, foolish, clown-faced. She cleared her throat. "Try a little posting trot to loosen him up a bit!"

In a moment she shouted, "Very good!" and Peter looked up startled at the pleasure in her voice. She was beaming on him. The hand shading her eyes seemed as much for the sake of protecting the world from their brightness as of protecting them from the sun. He sat up straighter and shortened his reins. MacDougal pulled his lips back and champed his teeth on the bit, but he did not seem to want to misbehave and Peter sensed this precisely, as if his body were a seismograph. He looked again at Kate, feeling for a moment that he of all the family was about to learn a lesson that she had to teach.

Peter, too, newly appreciated the slower gaits today. Any other exercise would have seemed sudden, clamorous. At the walk and trot he was beginning to feel his senses open up and mesh with one another. This, while it excited him, also frightened him; he had not expected to achieve anything for some undefined but proper number of months after John's accident. A plateau in his progress, if not downright retrogression, was what he owed to the fraternal relationship, but this improvement, he thought, must be part of the lesson, part of the reason that he and she were out here, active in the sun, and the others were hidden away.

"Take him over the wall," she called. "You look beautifully collected and in control."

There was not an inch of this training field that he did not know, where he did not have a dim or a clear memory of fright or hesitation. The stone wall was in a dip. How precipitous the incline had seemed when he was twelve, galloping around on Fried Pie and yearning to grab the pommel of his saddle. Now, on MacDougal, his approach, his response, his recovery were perfectly smooth. He turned toward the barrel jump. Kate, he knew, had not always liked him, perhaps had not liked him for the majority of his life. In the past, when he was praised for his schoolwork and received high grades, her eyebrows lifted, skeptically, doubting, with this evidence, the quality of the school. On horseback he had often exasperated her with the fog and slowness that he too found so exasperating but so uncontrollable. And he was no less tall these days, no less wincingly clumsy at times. Henry had always been the favorite, or perhaps John had been. Even Margaret, a few years ago, had taken every blue ribbon in sight and mother had treated her carefully, attentively. But now Kate was shining on him.

He took the barrel jump. It was perfectly pleasurable.

Perfectly pleasurable.

Just then it seemed that he had years to go before he neared the bottom of that pleasure, years of increasing strength and knowledge, years of books as well as horses, years of strategy and imagination, years of delight and fatigue and the renewable satisfaction of delight. Here was mother, a case in point, who had been around horses for almost all her life, and who still circled, tigerishly, this one pursuit. This, he thought, might be another part of the lesson that she had to teach him, knowledge of the unplumbable activity, the activity that no lifetime could encompass. He saw himself grown up, settling into an armchair, perhaps with a pipe, knowing what to do with his body, his hands, and his time, knowing that, however long he did it, he would always want to do it again, better. "Wake up!" she shouted, but her admonishment, as old as he was, was today light-hearted. He smiled, shyly at first, fearful of the gladness he felt. He wanted to be good. He always wanted to be good. His smile strengthened. MacDougal trotted briskly, flicking his ears and rolling his bits with his tongue. With a selfishness that felt like both victory and defeat, Peter took this happiness into himself and set up a guard around it.

Casually Kate stretched, then rested her palms on the top of her head. She was desperate with happiness and needed the matter-of-fact comfort of her hair and skull. Peter and Mac-Dougal soared over the barrels, then slowed to a trot, a walk, a halt. The horse dipped his chin and backed four steps, then, reins loosened, dropped his head and walked forward—light, graceful, ready for anything. They were very good, these two. They were very good, they were very good, they were very good. The Team, the Team, the Team. Before her she saw the product and goal of forty years of effort. On top of her head, her hands clenched into fists.

John, of course. But that boy seemed already small with distance, whereas Peter and MacDougal were enormous and growing, on the verge of eating her up. She thought of Peter on the Team, of Peter in Europe and South America. He need never be any better than he was right now and he would do well in those places. Her son, bone of her bone. They appeared together in her imagination, John in the highchair, strapped in because he had already wiggled out twice, and Peter perched on two telephone books, one bouncing and banging his tray table with his cup while squealing in time to his bounces, the other grave and already distracted, spiraling his peanut butter sandwich with careful half-moon bites. And she heard her own voice, chronically annoyed, saying, "Hurry up! Hurry up!" (she'd wanted to get on with her stable work). They had been, everyone said, darling little boys. The way that this memory dovetailed with her now frightening happiness and the glittering visions of Peter and MacDougal superbly accoutered amidst great green lawns felt like a disease of the soul. She gave a bitter groan and Peter turned Mac away, politely ignoring her.

She fixed her eyes on the weathervane atop the barn. Trotting west today. The little black horse trembled then, as the wind picked up, and knocked in its iron socket. With an effort of will larger than any of her willful life, she closed her eyes and ordered the images. When she opened them at last, Peter stood before her, and she wanted for him what she had always wanted for him, or someone, and the ground she stood on was hers again, again perfectly familiar through the soles of her oxfords. They circled and circled the training field, Peter on MacDougal, Kate usually at his side talking, often repeating herself. Twilight closed in on them, but the horse went around still, and the humans, without mentioning it, made no move toward the fragmented, stuffy, unbearable house.

On the screened porch, Axel, who could hear them sometimes, fell out of love with his wife and put his face in his hands. The darkness thickened. He went to the door and shouted, "Margaret!" but the house was silent and Margaret and Henry had disappeared.

"Margaret!"
She sat up instantly, opened her eyes even before she was awake, and said, "Yes? Henry?" without really knowing what she was talking about.

"I can't sleep."

"Wait a minute!" She spoke impatiently: the rising, the bundling together of her wits was so laborious, so slow. Henry stood quietly in the doorway, his pajamas glowing in the dark. "O.K.," she said at last. "Say, close the window, would you?" It had turned cool already. John, she remembered, was dead. Since the horse show, she had been waking from these deep, invertebrate sleeps to no knowledge, then to that knowledge, then everything else. Henry closed the window. When he sat on the bed, he had nothing to say, and Margaret had nothing to say, either, but it was reassuring to listen to his breathing.

John's accident, it seemed, had frightened them all speechless, speechless and embarrassed. It was a thought she had entertained before. (Lately she entertained lots of thoughts, layers of thoughts. Every feeling or perception nested in boxes inside boxes of speculation about why and how she felt and perceived. Nothing seemed to touch her deeply, except that it was impossible to stop thinking, and she had had menstrual cramps for nearly ten days.) There had not been much overt grieving from members of the family. If you saw soundless tears you did the person a favor and turned away. Mother, Margaret thought, would have preferred it even cleaner, would have preferred that, given his death, John had never lived at all. Then Margaret wondered again why the accident had rendered Kate so inhuman in her eyes, so that she could imagine her mother doing the most grotesque, unfeeling things, when actually she had simply done all the normal things: arranged for the funeral, gone to Mass, prayed, striven to achieve a semblance of normality around the place.

". . . run away," said Henry.

"Please don't."

"But I came back just then. At that very moment, I came back."

"What?"

"Well, really about ten minutes before, but it was almost right then."

"What are you talking about?"

"I said, I tried to run away that day, but I came back just in time."

"Where did you run away to?"

"I got to town. I had plenty of money, and a bunch of clothes and food and stuff."

"That's twelve miles from here."

"You're telling me." His back had slid so far down the wall that his neck, now at right angles to his body, looked broken. "Sit up," snapped Margaret.

He sat up, too preoccupied not to take orders, and went on. "I wasn't all that tired. I've been practicing since the beginning of the summer."

"Practicing what? What are you talking about?"

"Running away. I ran away. I've been riding my bike all summer, and I can ride up both sides of the driveway, and so when I got to town, even though it's twelve miles, I wasn't all that tired. I could have gone on for a long way. It was only noon, but I wanted to come back."

Margaret pulled the sheet up. "I should think so."

"Why? I had plenty of money and my raincoat and everything."

"I can't imagine your running away in the first place."

"You can't?" He turned and looked at her with completely uncynical wonder, and suddenly she could. In fact, suddenly it seemed like the most splendid, exciting, European idea, compounded of the sea and rain-washed golden pavements, and cozy perilous snowstorms remembered in comfortable old age. But she spoke skeptically. "Oh, come on. What would you do?"

"Make money."

"Sure. Doing what?"

"Anything."

"I'll bet." She was smiling, though, for in spite of her better judgment about high school diplomas and college educations, the thought had taken her over. She remembered John saying, "Margaret, don't you realize how many things there are?" and now she could see them: sailboats on sunlit oceans, avenues of shops, carved jades in velvet cases, aisles of books, rows of paintings, corridors leading from hospital rooms to labs to doctors' lounges. She imagined office buildings netted with telephone wires, whirring with business, and she thought of cool, dim, tableclothed restaurants where, at every place setting, the perfect food was being eaten. Henry said, "I can," and she said, "What?"

"Make money." He sounded so deliberative, so adult, that she looked at him suddenly. His pajama top was half open, buttons gone, no doubt, and she could see his chest, thin, smooth and cylindrical. His little ribs relieved and saddened her. She said, "Well, I guess you probably can, but you could make more of it if you finished your education."

"We'll see."

"Yes, we'll see." She made it sound like a promise, although what she was promising and how she would fulfill it she hadn't the least notion of. Still, with the thought of all those things that there were, all those places, and all those people with jobs, it seemed that any promise could be made, and that the mere making brought it closer to coming true.

Henry slid down the wall again and moved slightly away from her. Twice he opened his mouth, but closed it without saying anything.

"What?" she said, but he shrugged, muttering, "Nothing," and shaking his head. She smiled. He had made her happy. For the first time in days she felt happy. "What?" she said. "Tell me."

"You sound happy."

"Maybe I am. Talking to you makes me happy."

215

"Oh, yeah?"

"Yeah."

At this he moved even farther away, and averted his head entirely. He mumbled something.

"What?"

"I said, 'I don't think we should be happy.'"

"Maybe not," but this was not enough for him. He stood up. "Goodnight. Sorry I woke you up."

"Stop muttering and sit down."

He shuffled his feet and scratched his head, shorn of all adulthood now. "Come on, sit down." He sat down, but remained silent. With tact that made her feel deliciously competent, she waited. At last, panicked that he was about to cry, Henry uttered, "I missed him."

"We all miss him."

"I mean, I missed him then, when I ran away and got to town." His voice, shrinking from the mortification of tears, rose nearly to a squeak. "That's why I came back."

"What? I can't hear you." She put her hand on his knee and he pretended it wasn't there.

"I . . ." He took a deep breath. "I came back. *I came back.*"

Instantly she grabbed him and pulled his head to her chest. His hair, which mother had made him wash just before bed, was very fragrant, and she put her face in it. She could feel his tears running down her nightgown, seeping through and warming her skin. He was still talking, but she couldn't listen because the moisture seemed of such frightening, riveting intimacy. She felt it on her breasts, her abdomen, spreading, as if it would soak her whole body. And his body was shaking hers, his sobs wrenching her, as if by osmosis. She had done her crying, oddly, for months before the accident rather than since. These days she hadn't any tears left, and she did not feel guilty. Now, however, it seemed to her that she was crying by proxy, and she felt the emotions of tears: relief, embarrassment, the welling up of grief that grieves for itself as well as for the loss. She sat, holding and held, her face in his hair, for a very long time.

At last he was able to speak, and in a very sensible voice, as if he had not clung sobbing to some girl. "Well," he said, "it was really weird. I wasn't as happy about going as I thought I would be, but that was O.K. After I got started I was pretty hot, but I thought I would stop at the drugstore when I got to town, and then it would be afternoon and I could go some more after it cooled off. I didn't miss the horses or anything, or mom, or dad, or Peter, or even you, really." He looked quickly at her. "A little, maybe." She smiled and shrugged slightly.

"So I went to the drugstore and had a Coke and a doughnut and looked at the comic books for a while. I guess it was pretty neat to be in town by myself, except that I didn't have a lock for my bike and I kept having to stand by the window and watch it." He sniffed in spite of himself. "I had lots of plans. I mean, I was going to go down to the hardware store and buy a lock, and then maybe a Thermos, you know, and I thought about getting a couple of comic books to read in case I had to. I wasn't going to travel in the middle of days. They say that saps your strength, so I thought I would stop in some shady spots and stuff, and I thought I might want something to read then, and comics are very light and can be rolled up so they don't take too much room." He coughed. "Anyway, I was thinking about all that, and it was real hot, and I didn't really feel like doing anything. It was weird, because I hadn't been that tired when I got there, but then it just seemed liked every little thing was a big chore, so I had another Coke." He began to sniffle again, but fidgeted when she tried to touch him. She took her hand back to herself. "So anyway, I was sitting there and sipping my Coke, to make it last, and I asked the guy for more ice, and he gave it to me, and all of a sudden I started thinking about Jo . . . um, him, and I really missed him. I mean, he was pretty funny sometimes, you know?" Margaret nodded. Henry went on, with some difficulty. "But I thought it would go away, and just sort of kept sipping my Coke and kind of wiping my mouth to take up time. I tried to decide what comics to buy, and everything, and then I just got up and came home. And it was because I missed . . . I missed . . . And then . . ." He looked right at her, sucking his lips into his mouth and biting them in an effort not to cry. She nodded, and it was on her tongue to say that it hadn't happened, that John was asleep in his bed and would be there, grumpy and sarcastic, in the morning.

She shook her head, mostly at herself, but he took it as some sort of sign: the imminent tears dissipated in a deep, halting sigh, then Margaret wrestled into her mind the smooth, shimmering thought of all the things that there were, and said, "Yes, well, sit with me for a minute or so," but thinking of John, and Harrison, and everything else, she spoke so softly that Henry didn't even hear her.